Making Love Real

Making Love Real

The Church and
My Journey of
Mind and Spirit

The Reverend David McIndoe Hodges AM

Published by David Ross-Smith
Melbourne, Australia

Making Love Real: The Church and My Journey of Mind and Spirit
First edition published 2010
Second edition published September 2021
ISBN 978-0-6489508-0-6 (paperback)
ISBN 978-0-6489508-1-3 (ebook)

Copyright © David McIndoe Hodges, 2010, 2021

All rights reserved. This book is copyright. Apart from any fair dealing for the purposes of study, research, criticism or review permitted under the *Copyright Act 1968*, no part of this publication may be reproduced, scanned, stored in a retrieval system, recorded or transmitted in any form or by any means, electronic, mechanical, photocopying, recording or otherwise, without prior written permission of the publisher. Permission can be requested via email: davidshrs927@gmail.com

The right of David McIndoe Hodges to be identified as the author of this work has been asserted in accordance with the *Copyright Amendment (Moral Rights) Act 2000*.

 A catalogue record for this book is available from the National Library of Australia

Editing:
Anne McClelland (2010)
Maryna Mews, David Ross-Smith, Euan Mitchell (2021)

Layout:
Chris van Raay

Cover Design:
Luke Harris of WorkingType

Portrait:
Painted by Ellen Palmer Hubble (October 2010)

Photographs:
The Reverend Hamilton Aikin, Dennis Mayor, Jim Milne, David Ross-Smith

Music For David logo:
David Hubble

The money received from sales of this book will assist Uniting AgeWell's 'Music For David', a music program that supports people in their homes who are living with dementia, and gives temporary respite to their carers.

Let me not to the marriage of true minds
Admit impediments. Love is not love
Which alters when it alteration finds,
Or bends with the remover to remove.
O no! it is an ever-fixed mark
That looks on tempests and is never shaken;
It is the star to every wand'ring bark,
Whose worth's unknown, although his height be taken.
Love's not Time's fool, though rosy lips and cheeks
Within his bending sickle's compass come;
Love alters not with his brief hours and weeks,
But bears it out even to the edge of doom.
If this be error and upon me prov'd,
I never writ, nor no man ever lov'd.

Sonnet CXVI
William Shakespeare

Dedicated to my parents Jean and William Hodges who, in their love for each other, gave me the gift of my life and, in loving me, encouraged me by their example to live trying to make love real for others.

David in 1974 while minister of Toorak Presbyterian Church and Convenor of Presbyterian Social Services in Victoria

In loving memory of Peter Driscoll.

Contents

Foreword	1
Acknowledgements	9
Preface	14
PART ONE	19
1 Origins	21
2 Making Love	29
3 Love is a Confusing Word	35
4 Dreams and Disappointments	40
5 Law and Order; Love and Order	60
6 Towards an Agreed View of Human Nature	71
7 Theism, Hierarchies and the Churches	78
8 Religion and the Churches	83
PART TWO	89
9 Examining the Bible	91
10 The Fundamental Teaching	97
11 Adjusting the Gospel Setting	116
12 The Teaching of Jesus as a Way of Life for Today	123
PART THREE	129
13 The Experience of Wonder	131
PART FOUR	143
14 Reclaiming the Church as a Human Heritage	145
15 A Place to Start	149

16	Not a New Church but a Reformed One	157
17	Belief and Ritual	162
18	Living a Loving Life	167
19	A Spirit of Life Community	173
20	In Conclusion	176

Appendices	179
The Gift of Music	181
Memorials for David's Ministry	185
The Reverend David McIndoe Hodges AM, B.A. (Melb.), B.D. (Edin.)	193

Foreword

[2010 Edition]

CATRIONA MILNE

The story of the life of my father, David Hodges, has been evolving since 9 January 1924. My father has lived his life trying to make love real. As a young person, when I struggled to make decisions, he would say to me, 'The best way to judge if what you are doing is right, is to think whether it is the most loving thing you can do for the other people involved.'

This was not always easy to do. Sometimes I misunderstood him. I remember him saying that he wished to get to a stage in his life at which he did not need anybody. I mistook this goal for a desire for isolation from hurt and intimacy. When we discussed this years later, he told me he did not mean that he wanted to be completely self-sufficient, simply that he believed in inter-dependence and equality. Now, when he is so dependent and close to his own death, his capacity to be vulnerable and needy has taught me something else: to trust those who love you to hold you when you need it.

I said to Dad recently that I don't remember his ever telling me what to do. He may have when I was very little, but I have no memory of being controlled by him as an adolescent. In fact I remember saying to him, 'Please tell me what to do.' He replied as he usually did, 'What do you think?' He listened as I talked the problem through and worked it out for myself.

Another time he said, 'I trust you. I don't mean that I trust you to do what *I* think is right, because you will never know what that might be, but I trust you to do what *you* think is right.'

Dad used power in the way he describes in the book: to set others free. He used to say that I gave the same gift to my children. This book is another way of passing on that gift. It is the story of his journey. He describes how he developed his philosophy and how he tried to apply what really mattered in life.

He was not a saint: of course, he had imperfections. He describes these himself; we do not need to do so here.

His courage in pushing forward through major changes in his life is a testament to his belief in making love real. He said to me once, 'Trina — one thing I would say to you, don't make decisions based on fear.' He demonstrated this himself in continuing to honour the spirit of his marriage vows, while acknowledging his sexuality and giving up belief in a God who existed outside each human being. All this required remarkable courage.

He began to write this book in his mind about ten years

before he put pen to paper. He had been thinking more and more that to believe in a supernatural entity made no sense; in fact it was dangerous because it allowed people to give over responsibility for themselves and the world. I remember him saying, 'If we really knew that it was all down to us, we would take much better care of each other and our world.'

Dad ran study groups of like-minded people and wrote preambles to his discussions as food for thought. These evolved eventually into this book. He believed that he should get his thoughts down so there was integrity and honesty in his dealings with others. His whole working life had been about belief in God and he wanted to make sure that no-one was misled or in any doubt about what he had come to believe. He also wanted to share his thoughts and how he reached that point, thinking that it may be useful for others.

I have recently been listening to his sermons as a minister, and I learned amazing things that I never really knew before about my father. People always used to say to me, 'Your father is an amazing preacher — he has helped me so much.' Not unusually for a child of the manse, I never really listened to his sermons as a child. I was thinking about what we would have for lunch, or how I might spend the rest of my Sunday. Only as an adult did I get some idea of his gifts. He could tell a story and then take the listener to a place at which they heard for themselves something that helped them know how to live life at a profound level. He truly spoke to the core of what people needed. I didn't understand this until now and I'm so glad that we have this book which demonstrates this.

I hope you, the reader, find inspiration and love in these pages.

Austin Paterson

I thank David Ross-Smith and Catriona Milne for the opportunity to write briefly about David Hodges' influence on me and others. It is a privilege I could not pass up.

Over the years, David has had a profound impact on my life. He is a wonderful friend, a mentor and an extraordinary counsellor. He always has words of profound advice and I am enormously grateful that he came into my life when I was a teenager looking for purpose and direction.

When David was appointed as minister of Toorak Presbyterian Church, he quickly engaged with the Youth Group, which consisted of young people who were enthusiastic but without any real focus or leadership. I was fortunate to be invited with a few others to sit each Sunday evening in David's sitting room to map out a way forward for the older teenagers and young adults in the church, and for many others not really part of it.

The group became known as the Young Adult Group, which, as the 'YAGs', became a major feature of the outreach activity of the church. People of all ages and stages in the congregation involved themselves in ways that matched their interest. Under David's leadership, the YAGs brought older and younger people into the church with a shared sense of purpose and mission. I don't think I have ever seen anyone else achieve this with such skill and empathy.

One of David's biggest life-changing contributions was through quietly helping to guide and facilitate an outreach experience in the community of North Richmond High-Rise Estate, an economically and socially disadvantaged neighbourhood in inner Melbourne. For many years, up to eight members of the YAGs lived in a house in the community with financial support from members of the congregation. This opportunity enabled us to live and work with local residents in building a 'house' church in the flats, and to arrange and run family camps, youth programs, parent support groups, community health activities, to form a tenants' union and create many other initiatives.

We had a unique experience that led to strong relationships with local residents: many of these Richmond friendships continue to this day, forty years on.

David's influence on our development was profound. Never actually telling us what we might or should do, he guided us to think and plan far outside the normal square in a way that very few have had the privilege to experience. We all saw David as being larger-than-life and as an amazing trail-blazer. Through his guidance, leadership, mentoring and counselling, our group of young adults did so many life-changing and exciting things.

We developed confidence, a strong social justice perspective and leadership skills. In fundraising for worthwhile causes, we ran successful and entertaining reviews under the direction of Campbell McComas. Saturday night dances featuring Melbourne's best bands provided a safe place for up to 600 teenagers to go on a Saturday night; they became a significant part of Melbourne's night-life for many young people.

David's experience in running large-scale youth programs in Adelaide, prior to coming to Toorak, created confidence amongst our parents, who were in awe of this new approach in the activity and outreach of the congregation.

We learnt much about sharing and giving to others through activities such as creating performances at aged-care facilities. David's introduction and opportunities for discussion on religion and philosophy were vitally significant in our development as human beings.

Many of us, moving towards our sixties, are indebted to David for his influence and inspiration, and share an appreciation of his impact on our lives. We know that we would otherwise not be the same people. I, for one, am very grateful.

TIM BROWN

David Hodges is very special — gifted intellectually, socially, personally, spiritually and as a leader. He has more of each of these gifts than most. But no-one else I know is so blessed with all.

But there is much more to David than his gifts. His gifts have always been used in the service of others at the same time as he celebrates life in abundance. Such is the love and the aspiration that he describes here.

David arrived at Toorak Presbyterian (now Uniting) Church at the beginning of 1968, and I was lucky to greet him with my mother as the family arrived at the manse. Little did I know that, in the next year or so, he would baptise my wife-to-be, Catriona, start the Youth Group that shaped important, life-long friendships for me, and beckon to a life of commitment and fulfilment.

David has a powerful and wide-ranging intellect. His sermons at Toorak reflected his rigorous theological underpinnings and his sharp questioning of all dogma, at the same time as being a constant affirmation of his spiritual ideas. His constant challenge to the Youth Group, and subsequently to the Young Adult Group, was to question everything, but in the context of a clear commitment to underlying values. His sermons in the early 1970s encompassing creation, existence and biblical explanation remain with me today.

When David enters a room, the group looks up and relates to him. To describe this gift as charisma is to undervalue it. His social presence includes all people, affirms their worth and invites them on a journey. Perhaps he is unaware of the power of his social gifts.

David instinctively understands others and uses this to ask the right questions. He has shared this gift with me generously and for the great benefit of me and my family. It is impossible, therefore, to speak of his personal gifts with dispassion, but they are profound and have been used for the good of many. He seeks the truth, often intuits in advance of others, leading to surprising but beneficial outcomes.

Spiritually, David has wrestled with naivety and forged a response that many now follow. Embracing his Christian and Judaic heritage, he has sought to interpret the Gospel truths in new ways. Fear of innovation has not been dominant. Far from it — the spiritual journey to which David beckons us is one that will form and reform us all in the future.

David's leadership at Toorak and previously in Adelaide was a golden age for our group, the broader congregations and the wider Church. Large groups of people were engaged and drawn towards his challenging and compelling vision. For my group of friends, this led to friendships, attitudes and outcomes that have shaped our lives. On one day we were wrestling with ideas about creation and the social order in the privileged world at Toorak, on the next we were learning from those coping with harsher realities in Richmond. We were not alone in being led to experience constant new challenges and opportunities.

David has been the most important person in my life outside family. His combination of thought, spirit, word and deed has been as thoroughly pervasive as beneficial. He has been mentor, father-figure, counsellor and friend. In all, he has enriched and blessed me.

The ideas expressed here are worthy of study and thought. The life of David is shining and enriching — I hope you enjoy the textual reflection of this below.

Acknowledgements

DAVID ROSS-SMITH
[Updated 2021]

David Hodges' ministry was significant. It involved large numbers of people, not only in services of worship and activities for all ages within the Church, but in the wider community through social welfare and arts programs. Besides having a broad vision and being a skilled leader and administrator, he was also an excellent communicator.

In sermons and study groups, David used words, supported by sound scholarship, to clarify biblical teachings and make them relevant for contemporary living; in meetings, his words could inspire the development of projects or reconcile differences of opinion; when counselling, combined with his skills in listening, he would use words to help people work through their personal difficulties and conflicts; in times of grief and joy, his words gave appropriate comfort, support and encouragement. Although David died in January 2012, people still often address comments to me on the benefits they received from his ministry and preaching.

In 2005, at the age of eighty-one, David began writing down his thoughts on Christianity and the Church — a period during which he became aware of the onset of dementia. He was suffering from physical frailty and chronic pain, for which he was enduring heavy doses of medication. David gave his proposed book the title *Making Love Real*. In 2010, despite its appearing to be incomplete, his older daughter, Catriona Milne, and I were keen to publish what he had written. *Making Love Real* was launched by Catriona at that year's Christmas Soirée, one in the series of annual concerts held in David's and my home. The imposing portrait of him painted in October 2010 by our friend, Ellen Palmer Hubble, was also unveiled. It was entered in the 2011 Archibald Exhibition for portraiture and placed in 'The Hidden Faces' of the Archibald Exhibition. [See below.]

In 2013, the year following David's death, while researching material for *Love Made Real*, my book on his ministry at Toorak Uniting Church, I discovered three more chapters that he had written; and more recently, in 2020, additional material in a hard-copy manuscript of *Making Love Real*. All of these have been included in this revised edition. David put aside writing the book to record his family memoirs, which he titled *Family Story — Word Pictures*. Following a laminectomy in 2007 and subsequent further decline in his mental and physical health, he did not resume any form of writing. It is possible then that this edition of *Making Love Real* is still incomplete.

Acknowledgements

My thanks go to Catriona Milne for her enthusiasm for this project and loving memories of her father, and Austin Paterson and Tim Brown for those of their friend, David; Robyn Humphries and Marie Dalziel for their interest and help; Ellen Palmer Hubble for her artistry and keenness to paint David's portrait; and her husband, David, for designing a beautiful logo for the Music For David program; Eva Alegre for her patience and talent in enhancing old photographs; Anne McClelland for her literary skills and editing the original edition of 2010; Maryna Mews, with her wide experience in copyediting and proofreading, for editing this 2021 edition; and, finally, to Chris van Raay, with his expertise in layout and graphic design in creating the original book and this updated publication.

I am also grateful to those who have made contributions for inclusion in the Appendices: Tasma Wischer, for her gift with words; Catriona Milne and her sister, Jeannie Hodges, for their reflections on the creation of memorials to their father; Rebecca Ryan, General Manager, Marketing and Community Relations for Uniting AgeWell, and Registered Music Therapist, Winifred Beavers, for writing an informative account of Uniting AgeWell's Music For David program.

Finally, special thanks to Euan Mitchell and Luke Harris for preparing this book for publication. Euan, for his expertise and experience in editing and publishing, and Luke for his empathetic and imaginative cover design, and skillfully preparing the book for print publication.

It is appropriate that David chose *Making Love Real* as a title for his book. Throughout his life he tried to make love real for others, not only his family and friends, but anyone he met. Through this love he hoped to encourage them to be 'set free'. In publishing this second edition, I hope that we can further honour the life and ministry of my beloved late-partner, David: a tangible symbol of making love real for him.

David aged eighty-six — a loving portrait by Ellen Palmer Hubble.

Preface

DAVID HODGES

Do the Churches encourage or discourage a loving life? My conclusion is that while some individuals and groups within the Christian Churches have been inspired by the life and teaching of Jesus, which has made love real for themselves and others, the Churches as institutions have inevitably discouraged many in their search for a life that leads to this end.

Many authors dealing with similar issues write from an academic, theological or philosophical position, which does not make easy reading for those not familiar with these disciplines. The ideas I present here are expressed in the conviction that truth, when it is known, is essentially simple and accessible. They are expressed largely through the medium of my experience of more than thirty years of pastoral ministry, and the outcome of a great deal of study and reflection over and beyond that time. I argue that the causes of this situation can be traced back to the first century of the Christian Era, and that they arise from both a misunderstanding and a manipulation of the teaching of Jesus. The misunderstanding was influenced by the prevailing view of the nature of the world, which was a supernatural one. Human beings were understood as subjects required to obey or placate the gods. Events that were mysterious in their origin and their manifestation were attributed to supernatural power.

Judaism, the world of belief in which Jesus and the first Christians lived, had refined this concept and asserted that there was only one God and that Israel was a nation chosen by Him to be the instrument of His purpose. The life of the nation was built on the practice of laws given by God and implemented by their leaders. This belief is described as theism. The Christian Church emerged in that environment.

Theism requires and promotes the rule of law, the establishment of institutions and the creation of hierarchies. While it is not possible to clearly separate the accurate and edited versions of the facts of Jesus' life and teaching in the four accounts in the Gospels of the New Testament, I maintain that it is possible to establish its fundamental elements. His teaching is a clear contradiction of the rule of law as the inspiration of a loving life. While law is necessary to an ordered society, it inevitably promotes corruption. The leaders of the young Church adopted the concept of the rule of law and built its life on that foundation. Subsequent corruption has led to many reformations, but none has identified theism as the fundamental error. I argue for a rejection of that doctrine and its outcome — the institutional, legal form of the Christian Churches. It questions the assumption that while secular communities depend on law to maintain them, this also applies to the Church. Love, I maintain, creates its own order.

I am not proposing the creation of a new Church, but a radical reformation of the whole structure that dates back to the first century. In the final section, I indicate some of the marks, and the basic form, of such a reformation.

I conclude that while nearly all reformations, large or small, are initiated by theologians, priests and ministers, the next significant reformation of the Churches will be initiated primarily by educated lay men and women trained in a variety of disciplines who, looking for a fulfilled life, will find answers in many places and particularly in the teaching of Jesus.

*David at his family's celebration
for his eightieth birthday, January 2004.*

PART ONE

[Words in square brackets that are occasionally inserted throughout this book indicate additional information by David Ross-Smith.]

CHAPTER ONE

Origins

I have spent a good deal of my life trying to make love real. This is not to claim that I am special or have some particular virtue, but neither has it been accidental. It was the outcome of being brought up by parents who wanted to commit their lives to loving their neighbours as themselves. I, and my brothers and sister, being the neighbours closest to them, experienced the full force of that intention.

We lived in a developing residential area, one of a handful of homes surrounded by paddocks that were in the process of being obliterated by progress. Some of our extended family lived reasonably close and each weekend they would visit. Most of my mother's family lived further away and clearly felt that they had some sort of duty to ensure that we were well brought-up. On one occasion, when I was a child, I overheard a telephone conversation between my mother and one of her sisters in which I was being unfairly criticised. This was a challenge to the commitment to making love real, and created an early awareness in me that some people were not as lovable as others. This, however, was offset by my mother's defence of me — a confirmation that, although I thought she was a bit hard on me, she basically approved of me. I knew I was loved. I later became increasingly aware of her concern for the new young families who moved into the streets around us, and the affection she gave to these neighbours.

There was, however, a more encompassing, caring environment around us. The new community had two focal points. One was the Regent Theatre where we often went on a Thursday night. The other was the local Presbyterian Church, which we attended from infancy, not just often, but always on Sunday. It was the well-spring of our parents' concern for their own and their extended families, and their neighbours. They were natural Christians. They were also conventional Christians.

Like many of my generation, I was a 'good boy' — I mean that I was responsive to the loving environment surrounding me. I accepted that good boys should trust the example of their parents and elders. However, there was a seed of distrust sown in me when I was around the age of six. One of my vivid, and therefore significant, memories dates from that time. Towards the end of the first year at school, a few of us were talking about Christmas. Billy, the biggest boy in the group, laughed and said, 'You don't really believe in Father Christmas, do you?' At first no-one replied and he repeated the question. In our family we had been brought up as little children to believe in this loving visitor to our home, and I trusted my mother's

CHAPTER ONE   Origins

words. I asked Billy then how did the presents arrive, and was answered by, 'Don't be silly, it's your parents who do it.' To which I replied that it was not, and that if he didn't believe me, I would fight him for it!

When I arrived home that afternoon with a black eye, I had some explaining to do. When the story came out, my mother sat me down and said, 'In a way Billy was right. Dad and I do buy presents for you and there is no real Father Christmas who brings them. But, in another way, he was wrong. There is a real spirit of Christ — that's what we believe.' From that time and into the future, I went on trusting her. I believe that, as a good boy, I repressed this first doubt and learnt that having trust was a good way to deal with future experiences.

We were fortunate in our childhood and adolescence to have as a minister Eric Owen, a man who was lively and outgoing, with a gift for friendship and a very human understanding of the value of the life of the community. The gospel he preached and lived was embedded in the reality of the human life of Jesus. That was his ideal, and it flowered in the congregation in a great number of activities: tennis, football, scouts, guides, men's and women's groups, drama and plays, and a great range of teaching and discussion groups for children and adolescents through to the early adult years.

It was he who asked me, when I was about seventeen, to think about the ministry as a vocation. My first response was to say that I would consider it. I was certainly open to thinking about that sort of life, but I was also aware of a growing distrust of the Church at large. My father had become very involved in the wider Church and in its financial organisation. I remember the worries he would express occasionally about the institutional nature of the Church, which seemed to be alienated from that community of faith and love that was so great a part of his life. Looking back, I think I understand his initial dismay, some years later, when I told him that I wanted to become a candidate for the ministry.

However, in 1941, I was seventeen and Australia was at war. I, like my contemporaries, had other things to think about. I thought that I would enlist in the navy. In so doing, I could volunteer at seventeen-and-a-half and get on with the inevitable future I would encounter at eighteen when, in any case, I would be conscripted.

My father, although a quiet and gentle man, put his foot down and refused to give his necessary consent. So, in February 1942, at eighteen, only weeks after the attack on Pearl Harbor, I enlisted in the Australian army (A.I.F.). Our induction was at Royal Park in Melbourne. Only two of us in our company of soldiers had matriculated from secondary school. In the first week, we were both put in charge of a permanent army sergeant who drove us to Port Melbourne, where a cargo of armoured vehicles, destined for what was then the Dutch East Indies, had been diverted to Australia. All of the documentation was written in Dutch. We could only assume that, due to having

CHAPTER ONE Origins

matriculated, it was thought we should be able to read and understand this foreign language. We did our best and wrote the requested report.

At this time there were fears of an invasion of Australia by the Japanese army. A line stretching west from Brisbane was to be fortified and the armoured divisions were to be a major element. For most of the next three years, I was involved in the preparation and dispatch of armoured vehicles.

After finishing at Port Melbourne, I was posted to Bandiana in northern Victoria. One morning we were told that we were to begin bayonet training. We were marched to the top of a small rise from which we could see below us a row of stuffed sacks suspended from frames. On each sack was painted a realistic image of a Japanese soldier. Our instructor showed us the best way to insert, thrust and twist the bayonet and, in colourful language, encouraged us to relish the death of our enemies. This whole procedure shocked me. On that day I left behind my protected and privileged childhood and knew that I wanted my life to be committed to making love, not war, real.

These are the foundations, laid before my birth, in home and in the community of the Church, on which my life has been built.

As I faced my future at the age of twenty-one, there were fewer community opportunities in which to work professionally than there are today. In 1944, when it became clear that the war was moving towards an Allied victory, we were interviewed about our future intentions.

I said that I had decided to study for an arts degree in Melbourne, with a view to either teaching or ministry in the Presbyterian Church. I was unaware then that the Church would soon claim me as a candidate, and was discharged at the end of the year. I had doubts about identifying myself with the Church, even at arm's length, and finally decided that the only way to truly resolve my questions was to study theology.

David joined the Australian army in 1942 on turning eighteen.

CHAPTER ONE Origins

The outcome, after I finished an arts degree and the first year of a Diploma of Education, was to study theology. I left for Edinburgh and New College, The University of Edinburgh, in 1949 and embarked on a further three years of university and a Bachelor of Divinity. I found myself part of a world informed by some of the best Christian and academic minds of that time. New Testament scholarship, radical theological views and new friends who shared my hope of a brave new world gave substance to my desire to make love real. I found myself a member of a community which was united by a common belief and commitment that I had not experienced since childhood. Most of us were in our twenties and all of us had memories of war, some as participants, some in countries occupied by an enemy, some from bombed cities in Europe, some from neutral nations, all sharing a desire and a hope for a future shaped by love. I came to believe that the best contribution I could make would be through the community of the Church.

That was fifty-five years ago. In the past twenty, I have had the desire, the time and the opportunity to reflect on those earlier years. Now I have reached a point at which I understand much better why there have been many times that I have been inspired, excited and comforted by my life as a minister in that world of the Church where love is made real; but also acknowledge the frequent times when I have felt disappointed and disillusioned. This book is the result of that experience and a search to resolve the reasons for the duality in a life based on traditional Christian doctrine.

I went as a young adult to study theology in Edinburgh, in part to test my doubts about the institutional Church. Another factor in my decision was that I was sure my future lay in some sort of people-oriented occupation, and there were few opportunities available outside the obvious ones of medicine and teaching. My doubts about the institutional Church were far outweighed by the possibilities that it offered me — the experience encouraged me to minimise my fears and maximise my hope. As you read on, you will see, and I hope understand, the reasons that I, while maintaining my status in the Church, am no longer involved in its life.

This is not meant to be a historical or theological treatise, although many years of study lie behind it. It is, in part, the story of my life, one that is inextricably linked with the Christian Church, through childhood and ministry and into the years beyond.

I know that the claims that I and others make will be challenged, just as they challenge millennia of Jewish and Christian thought. I am more than a little daunted. However, I believe that I am not just a foolish and egotistical old man, but one for whom love has been made real through the many loving people by whom I have been nurtured.

I believe that essential truth is simple and must compel the attention and the assent of us all. The Gospels contain this truth — that the key to a fulfilled human life is in the continuous emphasis of Jesus' teaching, summed up in one of his last instructions to his friends: 'Love one another, as I have loved you.'

CHAPTER TWO

Making Love

[This chapter and the one following have similar thoughts. However, both have been included here for comparison.]

The term 'making love' has a common meaning in our society. It describes sexual activity between two individuals. Sexual coupling is one of the most intimate expressions of reciprocated love. It is also an activity that can express lust, domination or individual sexual pleasure without regard to the wellbeing or pleasure of a partner. A large majority would maintain that lust or domination is very clearly not motivated by love and would deny that they ever acted in that way. I think, however, that a significant number would, if truthful, acknowledge that self-gratification, without regard to the needs and desires of a partner, is sometimes an element in their sexual life. Without doubt, self-gratification or, more gently, the individual pleasure of making love is an appropriate and reasonable expectation. This expectation is in fact an essential part of our relationships as human beings. Love is realised and appreciated when it is equally returned. The process of establishing that balance is part of making love. It perhaps has its clearest expression in sexual love because one of the outcomes is the creation of children. Yet it is only one of the outcomes. It is a reminder that love must be viewed in its biological context, that it is nature's way of ensuring that the propagation of life is central to its continuation. Falling in love is, in that sense, a misleading description. Responding to desire may be more accurate.

However, this is not the end of the story. The first phase of this relationship has been described as a period of 'limerence', perhaps best thought of as a time when we are mutually absorbed. Observers and participants discover that limerence rarely lasts for more than two years. The next phase could be described as settling down. We are emerging from the biological imperative and desire is modified, hopefully transformed into a freely given commitment to partner, children, wider families, friends and acquaintances. The first principle in the business of making love as individuals becomes clear. It is that a balance of giving and receiving must be established. This applies to our relationships on all levels.

A great deal of our daily life is taken up in the exchange of services. For example, we directly support a postal system as part of our communication infrastructure by providing a stamp for our letters. We expect a return by receiving our mail in good time and in good condition. To achieve this, we are also asked to provide an adequate receptacle located within a prescribed distance from the

CHAPTER TWO Making Love

street. When a balance is achieved between the provider and the recipient there is harmony. This may seem a long way from sexual union, but the desired outcome of harmony is the same. This is admittedly an elementary way of making love real, of creating harmony.

An open, cooperative attitude towards those whose lives intersect ours, we call 'affection'. It is an important form of love and applies equally to casual acquaintances, friends, families and lovers. Creating and building a loving environment in a community depends on a feeling of affection for each other.

Friendship has a further dimension and involves the sharing of interests and making time to be together to enjoy them. Making love real in a family has an even wider dimension and a natural advantage in terms of time spent together. It contains elements of friendship but additionally of inter-dependence and nurture, while a shared heritage is an additional bond.

If it is true that love makes the world go round, it is also unfortunately true that its absence makes the world go pear-shaped. The enemy of love is fear, and fear is always lurking: fear of others who may hurt us; of those who might exploit us; of the loss of those we love; of economic insecurity; of not being loved or valued or respected — the list is endless. Jesus taught truly that 'Perfect love casts out fear,' but our human experience all too often falls short of that perfection.

Traditional Christian teaching, which I am challenging,

asserts that there is another way of loving that does not depend on a response being made, but is offered without any expectation of a return. This teaching maintains that, in Jesus, a love beyond these human loves was revealed and that his absolute love was not the gift of his humanity, but of his divinity. For us to love as he did, we must be open to and accept the gift of the Holy Spirit. The New Testament uses a word for this love which, while expressed through our humanity, does not originate in it. In Greek it is 'agape', which, to differentiate it from our English use of the word 'love', may be translated as 'loving kindness' or, with the original meaning of the word 'charity'. The injunction to love one another, or the assurance of the love of God for us, is not a matter of affection or friendship or sexual love, but of what can be described as loving kindness. This love does not depend on being reciprocated to be realised. If we do not experience reciprocated affection, friendship or sexual attraction from others, we are still capable, with God's help, to act towards them with loving kindness. When we embrace this possibility, it transforms our human loves and transcends them. Traditional Christian teaching maintains this is only possible when we believe in the God revealed in Jesus. If we want to see love made real — not only through our affection, friendship and sexuality but in a way that transcends these — where do we find the way to achieve it? Is the gift of 'agape' a divine or human one?

To approach an answer to this question, I want to consider another common term used by a wide variety of people in our own time. It is 'spirituality'. While its use often seems to describe an out-of-this-world experience, which is ambiguous, it is possible to see that behind the description is an awareness of the world we know in a new way, in a new light. It may be hearing music, watching a beautiful sunset, experiencing a sudden sense of happiness or peace. The world we know for a moment reveals itself in a special way and we give ourselves to that moment. Awareness exists in the space that lies between us and the other, the total environment that surrounds us. This space is not necessarily filled with love. We can create hate, envy, malice and fear between ourselves and any other. Because we are always in relationship to our environment, we are always living in a world of the spirit, of love and all its opposites.

Ascribing to a divine power the sole ability to fill this space with love and, by implication, denying it to humanity, is demonstrably false. Our loving may be imperfect, but that is not to say that it is unreal. We are not creatures incapable of giving our love without return, but aware humans on a journey. Jesus' teaching is that as we fill that space between ourselves and our world with loving kindness, our lives will be fulfilling.

In terms of our humanity, this is not difficult to realise between ourselves and those whom we naturally love and who love us. Jesus was careful to point that out, but he then added that we should also aim to love our enemies.

The characteristic common to our enemies is that they

frighten us. Most of us, from time to time, need help to deal with our fears. The greatest help is to be surrounded by love, the enemy of fear. One of my earliest childhood memories was of my fear when a violent thunderstorm seemed to burst immediately over our roof. We had a large, open but sheltered veranda. Dad picked me up and, holding me close, carried me out into the storm. He explained that the big clouds were colliding with each other, making the lightning-like huge sparks and shaking the rain out of them. In his arms and in his confident voice, I found fear banished.

It is those loving me individually and in communities who have helped me deal with my fears. Love like my father's in that moment was perfect, and his perfect love, as Jesus taught, cast out my fear. We are not able to be perfect in all our responses to the fears of others, but there are moments when we can be. We do not have to leave it to some supernatural power. We have that ability within ourselves.

CHAPTER THREE

Love is a Confusing Word

What do I mean by 'making love real'? What follows will, I hope, make that progressively clearer.

Briefly, however, I maintain that many things portrayed as love are in fact something else. Love is real when it is a pure expression of concern for another. It is confirmed and enriched when it is returned. Much of what passes for love is tainted by self-interest in all its forms. 'I love you,' or 'Do you love me?' can be as manipulative as a loaded gun. 'I am doing this for your own good' — for the family's good or the nation's good — is frequently tainted and corrupted by the self-interest that prompts it.

Many writers have pointed to the poverty of the English language when we consider the nature of love. We can commonly say that we love our partners, our children, our dog, football, ice-cream and almost anything that gives us pleasure. Obviously, we do not mean the same thing when we apply the word to our feeling for ice-cream and to our feeling for our children. It helps, therefore, to be more precise.

Affection
Affection is a form of love. If we describe people as affectionate, we mean that they have an openness to others, which welcomes them without particular knowledge, and displays some pleasure in meeting and possibly getting to know them.

Friendship
Thinking of someone as a friend involves a greater knowledge and sharing of interests. An essential ingredient of friendship is an ongoing growth of that bond. In our life as a member of a family, we also experience that relationship.

Sexual / Romantic Love
If we fall in love and become a lover, we experience a greater intensity and exclusivity in our relationship.

These loves are common expressions of our human nature and are universal. When we experience love in ways we have so far identified, we are acting individually. We can have feelings of affection, friendship and sexual love, but if they are to be realised, they must evoke a response from another.

Loving Kindness
There is another way of loving that does not depend on a response, but is offered without any expectation of a return. Traditional Christian teaching asserts that in Jesus

CHAPTER THREE Love is a Confusing Word

a love beyond these human loves was revealed, and that his absolute love was not the gift of his humanity, but of his divinity. For us to love as he did, we must be open to and accept the gift of the Holy Spirit. The New Testament uses a word for this love, which, while expressed through our humanity, does not originate in it. As explained in the previous chapter, there is another way of loving, 'agape', which does not depend on a response. To recap, the injunction to love one another, or the assurance of the love of God for us, is not a matter of God's affection or friendship or sexual love, but of something that could be called 'loving kindness'. This love does not depend on being reciprocated to be realised. If we do not experience reciprocated affection, friendship or sexual attraction from others, we are taught that we are still capable, with God's help, to act towards them with loving kindness. Embracing this possibility transforms our human loves and transcends them. Traditional Christian teaching maintains this is possible only when we believe in the God revealed in Jesus.

THE DIFFICULTY

The difficulty, of which many are aware, is that they experience the presence of loving kindness in their own and others' attitudes without any awareness of the prompting of Christianity or a supernatural force. This raises the question of whether these two views can be reconciled. If we want to see love made real, not only through our natural loves — our affection, friendship and sexuality

— but in a way that transcends these and overcomes our equally natural feelings of dislike, prejudice and jealousy, to name but three, where do we find the way to achieve it, if not through the gift of a supernatural God who has been revealed in a man, Jesus, and promises this power?

Looking for the answer leads us who are, or have been, traditional Christians into deep water. My conviction, and my contention, is that we have no need of the concept of a supernatural God to find this answer.

The concept of a supernatural God is called theism. The *Shorter Oxford English Dictionary* describes theism as: 'Belief in one God as creator and supreme ruler of the universe, without denial of revelation.' This is the foundation stone of the universal Christian Church, as we know it. Not only is it expressed in the creeds and doctrinal statements, but it is also deeply enshrined in the practice of worship, the hymns and prayers of the people.

I will claim here, and in more detail in later chapters, that the concept of theism is at the root of the practice of law, and that the institutional structure of the Christian Churches is an inevitable outcome. The Churches, as basically legal structures, are in continuous conflict with the central truth of the nature of love that is the heart of the life and teaching of Jesus. This claim does not imply that societies do not need to be ordered. Communities committed to common beliefs find a shared order in a shared life.

David with three of his nine grandchildren: (left) in 1987 with Sandy Milne; (right) in 2004 with Cameron Hodges and Ella Hodges.

CHAPTER FOUR

Dreams and Disappointments

One of the more unusual aspects of the life of a minister of the Church is the much narrower separation that exists between the private and professional life. Years ago, a friend of mine in Scotland became minister of a church in a small country town. When I asked what it was like, his reply was rather cautious. 'It's the sort of place,' he said, 'where everyone in the town knows by 11 am what the minister has had for breakfast.'

The other side of being loved and cared for by your people is that they know a great deal about you and your family. We all hope for times when love is made real for us and for others, but we experience times when it is not, which on both sides creates fertile ground for disappointment, disillusionment and often cynicism.

I am convinced that this, and more, is largely the product of institutionalism. All bodies, including congregations, are given a legal form with which all parties must comply. Fifty years ago, and even now I think, people expect three things from their minister. He or she should be a

CHAPTER FOUR Dreams and Disappointments

good preacher, a conscientious pastor and good with the young. It creates an image, a formulated ideal. Images are dangerous when people try to live up to them. Examples come easily to mind: an ideal wife, husband, father, mother, boy or girl; an ideal boss or worker; an ideal host or guest; an ideal teacher, doctor, accountant or policeman. It applies to every occupation and individual to some degree. When we are critical, the assumption behind our thought is that, in some way, others do not meet our image of them, of what we expect them to be like. Years ago, a magazine invited children to write about their mother on Mother's Day. Most of the entries centred on what their mothers did — her tasks in the home and looking after children. The one that impressed me was: 'My mother is a person too.'

I have said that images are dangerous. In our communities fulfilling them is praiseworthy and failing them is not. It is dangerous when fulfilling an image involves denying our innermost hopes and desires, and leads us to superficiality of emotions and actions. It leads to judgemental attitudes and a failure to be open to others. It removes love from the equation of our lives and substitutes obedience to conventions and rules.

In the Churches, those ministers who fulfil the image, who manage to meet the criteria, are thought of as successful — the congregation numbers grow and the finances increase. The focus is on popularity, numbers and the financial bottom line. This is fertile ground for argument and dissent, and the dream of making love real is disappointed.

One of the clerical in-words during my early days of ministry was to unkindly label some of our peers as 'PFs' — 'professional friends'. What this meant was that the love, friendliness, affection expressed towards those to whom they ministered was not genuinely felt — but expressed as a duty and to fulfil an expected image. It was not real. I am convinced that the reasons for this are not simple. They apply to many human relationships, both secular and religious, and are deeply embedded in the institutional form of Christian Churches.

In the last year of training for the ministry, we were told by our professor of pastoral theology that he believed some of us were primarily prompted by intellectual curiosity; some by a passion to set the world right; while others, he feared, were attracted by the social status the ministry conferred. If you doubt this final category, remember that this was not contemporary Australia but Scotland half a century ago, where one confectionary company labelled its bottles of barley sugar: 'For the Use of the Aristocracy, the Gentry and the Clergy'. But to return to the advice of the professor — which I think should have been given in the first year of our training, not the last — he said the fundamental reason for becoming a minister was, quite simply, that we loved people.

I want to relate some memories of occasions when my dreams have been realised through love being made

CHAPTER FOUR   Dreams and Disappointments

real, and disappointed by others frustrating this outcome. You will notice that they have a common theme. The frustrations are generated by the forces of convention and regulation. These vary from unformulated social attitudes to formulated rules and codes of law — but they all favour law over love. Favouring law leads to the creation of hierarchies, which, in turn, lead to the establishment of bureaucracy. As participants in the chain of control, individuals find significance and the dangerous satisfactions of imposed power. These situations occur, not only in established structures, but informally in what we commonly describe as 'pecking orders'.

These memories span more than half a century and every congregation I have ministered to as student, assistant and inducted minister. Looking back over the years of my ministry, I am conscious that many of my dreams have become realities. However, my disappointments have led me to a new view of the Church. There were many more experiences than I describe here, but those that follow are, for me, important indications of the thinking that has led me to this point. I believe that my experience and conclusions are fairly typical of those of many faithful men and women who have left the Churches.

EDINBURGH

During part of the time I was in Edinburgh, I was a student assistant at St Giles' Cathedral, The High Kirk. Many people know it. Standing in the Royal Mile, just below the castle, it is located in one of the oldest parts of the city. Fifty-five years ago, the parish included one of the city's poorest areas, typified by tenement buildings. There was a clear separation, welcomed by both sides, between the local parish and the national church communities. One of the indications of the separation was the existence of a Ladies' Guild in the latter, and a Women's Meeting in the former. The student minister worked in the local parish, but was closely linked to the Sunday services in the kirk. Three of his responsibilities were to work with the Sunday school, conduct occasional funerals and visit in the parish. Visits, I was told, were not to last more than fifteen minutes and that thirty-five to forty were to be accomplished in a week. Regular visits were reserved for other days when the front parlour would have been suitably prepared. It was a punishing schedule and it is not surprising that when there was no-one home, I would heave a great sigh of relief.

The first funeral I took stays vividly in my mind. I was told that it was not customary to visit the family beforehand and that, if I did, it would be mutually embarrassing. Being a very small cog in an imposing institution, I followed instructions. On the day of the funeral, I made my way to the address and, many floors up — after passing a tap and toilet at every second level — knocked at the door. The man who opened it said, 'Good morning, Minister. Would you like to see Mother?' I thought that I had been told that it was the mother who had died, but thinking that I had

CHAPTER FOUR   Dreams and Disappointments

got it wrong and it must have been Father who had died, said, 'Thank you, yes.'

The door opened onto the single room in the home, and the twenty or thirty people gathered there suddenly became quiet. The son led me to a curtain drawn across what I assumed to be a window, but, when it was drawn aside, a bed built into a wall cavity was revealed. Mother was laid out on the bed. I turned towards the people and said something like, 'This must be a sad moment for you all.' The immediate response was for all to break out in a ritual wailing, during which four men came forward and lifted her from the bed and carried her to what I now saw was a coffin at the other side of the room. The wailing went on and I found myself drawn into the moment, tears welling in my eyes. The wailing suddenly stopped and every face turned to me. Obviously, it was time for me to begin the service. I stumbled through the words and we eventually got to the end. I had participated in the ancient ritual of 'coffining'.

The next day I reported my humiliation and failure to my boss. Dr Charles Warr was the minister and also the King's senior chaplain in Scotland and Dean of the Thistle (whom I, with others, behind his back, affectionately called 'Charlie').

'It's a good lesson to learn early in the piece,' he told me gently but firmly. 'You can't really help people if you stand with them in their grief. It's our responsibility to stand apart and lead them beyond that moment to where we are.'

I have been grateful ever since for that advice, but I have also become aware of its dangers. To remove yourself, as it were, from a moment like that, to become objective, is to risk losing the gift of empathy: to frustrate the flow of love and its healing power when it has the potential to become real. I have tried to come to the many funerals that I have conducted quietly and calmly, but at the same time remaining open to share the distress and grief that is present; to clear a way for the healing power of the spirit of love to be felt.

At the centre of what I am trying to express is the deep division between the exercise of law and the expression of love. To live by regulation and law, to legislate the time to be given for a pastoral visit, to conduct a funeral service through a fixed ritual, a formula in which one fits all, is to live by law and adopt an attitude that can form a great barrier to our desire to make love real in our own and others' lives. Law is a necessity in maintaining order in life but, as St Paul reminded the young Church in Rome, it is a 'murderer'. Law is a destroyer of empathy and love.

The Christian Churches, despite many challenges, have never freed themselves from the institutionalism that is essentially based on law and regulation. It is essential to remember that the first Christians were Jews who inherited the Law they lived by. One of the great struggles in the first century was between Paul, the missionary to the Gentiles on the one hand, and James and the leaders of the Jerusalem Church on the other. The clash between

CHAPTER FOUR   Dreams and Disappointments

works and faith, between law and grace, is clear in the New Testament.

However, I also believe, despite this fact that the universal Christian Church still holds for me a truth about the life to which I want to commit myself. For over thirty-five years, I was a parish minister. Now, twenty years after I retired from full-time ministry, freed from the commitment I gladly made, there has been time to reflect on these things.

St George's, Edinburgh, was, and is, one of that city's premier churches. In my time at St Giles', a new young minister from the Highlands was inducted at St George's. He was very popular. One very public dispute he had with his Session, the governing body, was about retaining the pews to which families, who paid for them, had exclusive access. Sundays saw long queues standing in the street, waiting for entry and the young minister wanted unrestricted access to every seat. Established families objected. He commented that their attitude reminded him of 'the moribund orthodoxy of the Highlands'. The word spread, of course, to the Highlands and the argument rolled on. In the end the position he took was vindicated and pew rents were abolished. I admired and loved him for the way in which he ministered with care to each side of the dispute. He had his own way of dealing with it. His first son was still an infant in his pram and would chuckle every time anyone he knew tickled him under his chin. His father developed his strategy. He would address his infant son with the question, 'And what do you think of the moribund orthodoxy of the Highlands?' and then tickle him under his chin. He was rewarded, as were his friends, by a delighted chuckle. It was, however, a very serious business.

When I was later inducted into my first parish, Bairnsdale [Victoria, Australia], he was able to be there. He completely stole my limelight, but his love left no room for anything but joy.

At St Giles', at an early meeting with the parish Sunday school teachers, one of the older ones asked me if she could have a word with me afterwards. She had a specific concern. 'It has always worried me that we speak about God as Father. I have spoken to the others about it, but some don't agree with me. I know that it is in the Bible, but I also know that many of these children have no fathers, and those who remain are often drunk and violent. To speak of God as Father simply frightens them.' From that time on, I spoke only of Jesus, the man of love.

Melbourne

When I returned to Melbourne to become the assistant to the minister of Scots' Church in the city, one of my early experiences was to be involved yet again in the subject of pew rents, which were still in force. My most vivid memory of the discussion about their abolition derives from a Session meeting. A former well-known politician and an elder of the church, red-faced, thumped the table aggressively and

CHAPTER FOUR   Dreams and Disappointments

shouted, 'My family has had our pew for generations and I have no intention of giving it up now!' There was very little sign of love made real around the divided table on that night.

I enjoyed visiting older members of the congregation. I remember clearly a visit to a woman who, when I arrived, was seated at a desk in her hall. She asked me if I would mind waiting for her to finish the note she was writing. After a minute, as she stood up, she said that it was a thank-you note and went on to say, 'I have always believed that one word of praise achieves more than nine words of blame.' I told my mother because I was aware that she had known her. When my mother died, many years later, and I was going through the few papers she had not thrown away, I found a card from this woman thanking her for her help when, as a girl, she had met and guided her to a meeting at her church. She had kept it for over seventy years.

There was a woman in the congregation who many thought was eccentric. She took every opportunity to attend study and discussion groups. She disliked St Paul and his letters in the New Testament, and claimed that he was distorting the clear message of the Gospels. I, in my youthful enthusiasm, often took issue with her. She did not appreciate it. After eighteen months I accepted a call, an invitation, to St Andrew's in Bairnsdale [a town 280 km east of Melbourne]. At my farewell, where many people were saying appreciative things, she stood up and made her well-known views even clearer. She concluded with, for me, these unforgettable words, 'Well, you're going. You'll empty Bairnsdale and what's more you'll empty Buchan too.' A bit eccentric, yes, but I wish she were alive to read this and to know that, not too late, I have moved nearer to the heart of the matter, as she had. We both came to the realisation that in the life and teaching of this man Jesus, we had seen love made completely real.

BAIRNSDALE

In Bairnsdale both dreams and disappointments continued. The congregation had experienced a very difficult time. My predecessor had roused strong opposition from many, including a number of the elders, the leaders of the congregation. They declared their position on communion Sundays, important quarterly occasions, by attending another church in a nearby town. I nervously set myself to heal this rift.

It soon became clear that the man who had led the dissent was no happier with me. Nearly everything I proposed was either openly — or more subtly — opposed. At the same time, I was aware that there were others who were strongly supportive, but apparently reluctant to risk another split. I began to think of him as an enemy. I was shocked not only by the situation but at my response to it. I believed that I had an equal obligation to care for him as for others in the congregation, but didn't know how to act. Finally, I decided that I had to try to resolve the matter and asked him to meet with me. I simply told him how I felt and that I did not know how to deal with it. When he didn't immediately respond, I said that if I honestly wanted to do something, I must learn how to love him as an enemy. He seemed as shocked to hear that as I was to hear myself saying it. I think that must have been where we left it, because I can't remember any more. What I do remember is that my anger disappeared and, although we were never close, the opposition also gradually ceased.

After some time, I invited all, and particularly those who were younger, to join a group preparing for confirmation and Church membership. The response was overwhelming and the class very large. In those days, the congregational contribution to the Church's central state Assembly, called the Budget, was calculated on a per-capita membership basis. One Sunday evening, as this group, mostly young, emerged from the hall, a member of the board of management, which was responsible for the finances, was there to close up for the night. He asked me who all these people were, and I told him, enthusiastically, that they were the membership class. 'Gawd,' he said, 'up goes the Budget!' He was a good and faithful steward, but money was paramount. A memorable story and funny in its own way, but no part of my dream to see reconciliation, love made real, in that community.

Much more seriously, a young woman whose family was associated with the church was murdered in the town. In a small community, everybody knew and most speculated about this tragedy. Her parents asked me to conduct the funeral service for her. Naturally, they were distraught.

In a way, they wanted everything to be private, but knew that this could be misunderstood and misinterpreted. They decided that the service should be held openly in the church, but asked that the coffin not be there. That, they said, would be too difficult for them to deal with. In small country towns, as Bairnsdale was in those days, conforming to community expectations, including funeral service conventions, was very important. Such a move would be exceptional. Nevertheless, I felt that the family's wishes and needs were paramount and it was arranged that the coffin remain in the hearse outside the church during the service.

A few days later one of the elders came to see me. He was a retired farmer and very wise. He came straight to the point, asking me if I had heard any comments about the funeral. The only specific response to me had been from her parents, who had told me how comforted they had been by an occasion they had feared. 'Well,' he said, 'I thought it best to tell you before anyone else did, that you are being accused of refusing to have the body of a murdered girl in your church.'

I assured him that I had not, and asked him what he thought I could do about it. He told me that he wouldn't suggest that I ignore it, and then said, 'Can I tell you what I think?' When I told him that I felt hurt and angry, he agreed that he would feel the same. He then went on to suggest that the rumour was based in anger that the murder had occurred — the very fact of its having happened had

CHAPTER FOUR Dreams and Disappointments

disturbed them all. The critics' reaction came, he believed, from their need to find something or someone to blame. They had settled on the minister. 'What you can do is to understand and accept what has happened and then go on loving us even more,' he concluded.

One of the truly faithful, loving and supportive people in that congregation was an older woman. She had married late and she and her husband were devoted to their son, a much-loved only child. At the age of twelve, he contracted infantile paralysis. He was seriously ill and, despite all the efforts of his doctors, nurses and family, he died one morning in his mother's arms. She told me that, when she had gently laid him back on his bed, she walked out alone into their garden. She said to me, 'As I stood there, I heard music. It was *Finlandia* [melody from a work by Sibelius]. I knew the words of the hymn set to it and I heard those too.'

> Be still, my soul: the Lord is on your side;
> bear patiently the cross of grief and pain;
> leave to your God to order and provide;
> In every change, He faithful will remain.
>
> Be still, my soul: when dearest ones depart
> and all is darkened in the vale of tears,
> then you shall better know His love, His heart,
> who comes to soothe your sorrow, calm your fears.

She had known fear made real. But their son was both a symbol and the reality of their love made real. Nothing could destroy that. Today, I would maintain that the source of her grace and her courage was the love she had known from her son, her husband and her friends. She led me, her young minister, and many others, deeper into the experience of love made real. Fifty years on, I continue to treasure her memory.

Adelaide

Following Bairnsdale, I became the minister of Scots Church, Adelaide, through most of the 1960s. It was the time of the Beatles' visit, street gangs and student unrest, all of which created a lot of anxiety in the community. My colleague and I decided that we should do something about this, and devised a program we called 'Sunday Night at Scots'. It began with a short service in the church, in a form that we thought would be attractive to our own young people and their friends, followed by opportunities for dancing, discussion, counselling and supper. Their parents and the older members gave us great support.

Some of the young ones, who at weekends roamed the city streets in general and North Terrace in particular, saw that something was going on and decided to join in. We had organised the evenings in such a way that anyone who came had to be involved from the beginning of the program. There was to be no gate-crashing for

CHAPTER FOUR Dreams and Disappointments

the dancing only. Gradually, the scene changed. The smart informal appearance of the group gathered in the church began to become more obvious on one side, while the other side became equally defined by torn jeans, tee-shirts, belts, buckles, chains, all topped by long hair. This was real.

In the regular congregation, the alarm was sounded. This was Scots Church, the city church of Presbyterianism, opposite the university and Elder Hall, named for its benefactor who was also a prominent Presbyterian in his day. We now had the spectacle of the Adelaide Police Anti-Larrikin Squad regularly parking in beautiful North Terrace near the church. The protest, as was so often the case, concentrated on the long hair of the participants in our program.

One Sunday morning, arriving early, and entering through the main entrance, I saw, propped up on an easel, an enlarged photograph of a minister in his clerical dress. I recognised him immediately. It was of Dr Black, the minister of St George's in Edinburgh, taken many years before. He was ultra-conservative. I had no idea who had arranged the placing of this portrait, but I immediately saw why. The photograph clearly showed dark, flowing hair cascading over his deep, white clerical collar and his shoulders! I later learned of the gracious, elderly grandmother who was responsible. The photo stayed there just long enough for the long-haired young to enjoy and the outraged reaction of the objectors to subside.

A little later in the program, many lively discussions took place. We all sat on cushions around the walls. Once, as I went in, I saw four young, short-haired men in suits sitting in the group. The early details of the ensuing conversation I do not remember, but eventually one of the young visitors asked me a question. 'Do you think that what you are doing is leading these young people to salvation?' I replied, heart in mouth, that it would be better if the ones who were there answered for themselves. One of them, known (for obvious reasons) only as Scruff, spoke up. 'Of course, it is. We used to come into town every weekend looking for cars we could take for a ride, and if we couldn't open them, we would just bash them up. Now when we come into town, we think twice about that.'

The four very decent young Lutheran theological students, I am sure, went away shocked but thoughtful. Scruff, if he is alive, must be in his middle fifties now. I would love to know if that first new impulse finally brought him to a point where love was made fully real for him.

Toorak

My next and last charge was the then Toorak Presbyterian Church in Melbourne. By this time, 1968, I had travelled a long way from the youth and young minister who had repressed his suspicions and doubts about the institutional nature of the Church. During this period, I had found myself more and more deeply committed to the teaching of Jesus and the building of a loving community of faith.

CHAPTER FOUR   Dreams and Disappointments

Toorak seemed to offer me the opportunity to be part of that.

However, on my second or third Sunday, the morning service was drawing towards its close when I saw one of the managers-on-duty standing right at the back of the building. He was a very successful businessman. He was holding up his left arm and with his right-hand index finger pointing to and tapping his watch. After I had farewelled the last ones to leave, he walked up to me and said, 'We always finish the service within an hour. You were five minutes over time this morning.' I later became acutely aware that part of his success as a businessman was his obsession with the need to make efficiency real and using his authority to do just that.

As I reached the front gate of our new home that morning, my four children rushed up shouting, 'Hurry up, Dad, you're on telly.' What they were watching was a televised recording of a recent service in Adelaide. As the camera moved over the faces of the congregation, I saw some I had come to love through sharing their sorrows; others whom I had married and whose children I had baptised; many who had always greeted me with a warm smile and taught and inspired me through their loving care — all, and more, whom I had left to come to a new place. Suddenly, I longed to be back there.

One of the first decisions was to form a small group of interested and committed people to prepare a plan for the future. It was taken for granted that the programs of worship, education and pastoral care would continue. But beyond that, the focus would be on directing the resources of the congregation to meeting the needs of the community of which we were a part. A day kindergarten had operated for years. Subsequently, three other centres were established. One was for family life and support; another for the care of the elderly; and the third, a centre for the arts, to extend and deepen the life of the congregation, and to invite the wider community to use the facilities that we enjoyed.

Fifteen years later I left Toorak where both dreams and disappointments continued and where, again, I was supported by many loving people. Now, another twenty-two years later, I pay tribute to all those who have made love real for me. Jesus' teaching and example was the inspiration. That is our one calling, to try to make love real for our world.

David at Toorak Presbyterian Church prior to the creation of the Uniting Church in Australia in 1977.

CHAPTER FIVE

Law and Order; Love and Order

A Legal Perspective

Societies are formed by individuals who share a common connection in an occupation, an interest, or some aspect of identity. It is acceptable in these terms to speak about an Australian society, a stamp collectors' society, or even a criminal society. There are qualifications to membership defined by the nature of the connection. To be an Australian, for example, it is necessary to fit one of the criteria that are set out in Australian law. Communities, on the other hand, while they may be regulated, are built around individuals who hold common values that apply to their whole life, not one part of it.

On a national scale, there are the examples of the emerging European Union and the various national interests that conflict with it. On a world scale, the drive towards globalisation meets with both violent and concealed opposition. On a local scale, the growing support of sports groups, some of which have a common

CHAPTER FIVE   Law and Order; Love and Order

ethnic interest, can lead to violent adulation in victory and equally violent behaviour in defeat.

There exists, in some cases, difficulty in distinguishing between society and community groups. This occurs when the cohesive factor is a limited interest that becomes total. For some, the limited interest dominates their attitudes and actions. These individuals may become committed to each other in the pursuit of their common interest. We would normally think of them as extremists. The danger that lurks in the life of every community is the divisiveness that leads to eventual destruction.

This is more prevalent in the so-called free Churches, and one of the most obvious examples is the periodical emergence of fundamentalism. One form, with which most Christians are familiar, is a belief that every word in the Bible is the unalterable word of God. However, within this, there are a number of variations. For example, some who find absolute grounds to oppose divorce would not support the theory of creationism that supports the literal truth of the biblical account in Genesis.

The teaching and life of Jesus illustrate that fundamental love is essentially inclusive. He was vehemently opposed to the law of his day, which was extreme in its purpose to maintain the nation's uniqueness. All law then and now is divisive, 'separating the sheep from the goats'. The Christian Church in its adherence to the way of law is fundamentally flawed. This becomes obvious when a group defines itself within a congregation, or any other organisation, by its difference from the main body. In the Churches, in the past and sometimes still, this is finally resolved by a heresy trial, by ex-communication or by other legal definitions. In a legally defined organisation, this often results in the re-defining of membership rules, which are stated as laws, or by the leadership ignoring those who question, and hoping that their attitude will lead to voluntary withdrawal. Of those who are left, some are happy to see them go and find their prejudices reinforced. Others are led to consider whether they find their own membership weakened and questionable. I believe that this is one of the main reasons for the rapidly diminishing membership of the Christian Churches.

Any community, in order to define itself, requires an understanding of its nature by its members and the nature of their participation in it. This process will be varied and will lead to many forms of regulation. These will include, at one limit, the formulation of a legal system based on precedent, the means to create new laws to meet changing circumstances, and the maintenance of the whole system of policing, of courts and of the rehabilitation and/or punishment of offenders.

At the opposite limit, a relationship between two individuals in a life partnership will define itself by the elements of its existence, both for the participants and for those who observe them. This will not be maintained by any external factors, but by the internal desire and willingness of both to continue in the relationship.

CHAPTER FIVE Law and Order; Love and Order

Between these two limits, there are many variations in the formation and ordering of communities. Generally, the wider the boundaries of the environment of a community, the greater will be the need and the call for 'law and order'. We all live within national boundaries, and the exercise of law to maintain order, therefore, has a major effect on our behaviour. If we willingly accept the need for the operation of law in our daily lives, we can live with reasonable comfort within its restrictions. If we decide to live in ways that are against the law, our comfort zone may be reduced. Basically, however, both decisions are motivated by fear that, if we break the law and are discovered, we will suffer. Fear admitted to any part of life quickly invades the whole.

One of the difficulties many otherwise law-abiding individuals encounter arises when the line between public and private behaviour is invaded. An example is the legislation covering marriage and de facto relationships. Marriage in Western culture is a relationship between a man and a woman, which is defined and regulated by law. The eligibility of participants is established and celebrants must be registered. [Since David wrote these words in 2005, there have been changes to this law in a number of places throughout the world. For instance, marriage equality was made legal in Australia on 9 December 2017.]

Although this aspect is simple, the legal dissolution of marriage is not. In Australia before the early 1970s, the grounds for divorce were complex and often challenged. Many of the laws were regarded as invasions of privacy.

This resulted in a major change to what is known as 'no fault' divorce, where couples who file for divorce have only to establish a separation from their partner for a period of a year in order to have it legally granted.

The question also arose concerning those who were not legally married but had lived together for some time as though they were. These then were legally defined and in the case of separation, the distribution of shared assets and the treatment of children of the couple, the law was extended and refined. Some of those who have not been legally married see this as an invasion of their privacy.

Subsequently, the question has been raised about same-sex partnerships. Comparatively recently, they were illegal until anti-discrimination laws were passed. The result of that development has been to create a great deal of confusion as to whether they should be regarded as equal to de facto marriage relationships. In all of this, the personal, financial and property rights of individuals have to be considered. Again, some would advocate new laws, while others would oppose them on the grounds of individual privacy.

This one example of the blurring of the line between public and private behaviour is enough to illustrate the difficulty of legislating to order and control it. It also demonstrates the inevitability of the elaboration and extension of law in society, together with the subsequent growth of corruption and the invasion of fear in our lives.

CHAPTER FIVE   Law and Order; Love and Order

A Loving Perspective

Love for another, whether it is expressed as affection, friendship, family or sexual love, cannot be created by law. It is an inward attitude to others that is created by a mutual decision between individuals. This relationship will not be maintained by any external factors, but by the internal desire and willingness of all to continue in it.

To illustrate this, we can consider life in the community of a family. When parents and children act lovingly towards each other, there is harmony and no need for imposed authority. All the family members, particularly as the children develop, become disciples and there is no need for imposed discipline. Order is the outcome of commitment to loving one another. This may seem to be a counsel of perfection — even in the most loving families there will be occasions when parents will feel the need to 'lay down the law'. A lot depends on whether this is the rule or the exception in that family's life. If it is the rule — the principle of order in family life — it will develop into a legal entity and define standards of behaviour in all areas, which may not be recorded but will certainly be understood by all. If it is the exception, when discipline is exerted, accompanied by consideration of all the individuals involved, a deeper mutual understanding and acceptance of the way of love can result.

A difficulty encountered in maintaining a separation between the ways of law and love is to clearly identify what I describe as instrumental and intimate relationships.

In the former, there is a contract between two parties to act responsibly towards each other. It can be, as I have described previously, as simple a thing as a postal system. A great number of our day-to-day relationships are instrumental and appropriate, and should not be dismissed as inferior. They can, and do, promote harmony and enjoyment.

However, one of the ways in which living by law slips under our guard is to settle for personal instrumental relationships when intimate, loving ones are the appropriate basis. This occurs when we strike bargains with those we say we love. These bargains are often unspoken, but what lies behind them is an instrumental relationship: 'If you do what I expect and want, I will be satisfied.' This is foreign to the way of love. Where love commits, law contracts; where love forgives, law seeks redress; where love trusts, law asks for obedience. Living becomes a process of bargaining, not of making love real.

Another more subtle but common way in which unwritten law slips under our guard and damages love, is in the area of morals — attitudes and behaviour that are concerned with what we think of as right or wrong, good or bad. This is an area where prejudice flourishes. It exists both within and beyond the scope of law and is generated by individual attitudes often based on personal experiences or limited knowledge. It is revealed in statements like: 'All gypsies are thieves' and 'All politicians are corrupt.'

As I am writing [July 2005], London has suffered a

CHAPTER FIVE   Law and Order; Love and Order

terrorist attack. It has been established that those who carried it out were adherents to Islam. One of the reactions has been to hold all Muslims responsible. This is prejudice in an extreme form and, thankfully, will not be supported. But there are still those who will think that the bombing was justified. I am not advocating that we should not make judgements, but I am maintaining that, in many instances, what we claim to be good and right can, in fact, be bad and wrong.

What is called the 'ethics of choice' further illuminates this situation. When we are confronted with any decision about our behaviour, there are only three possible choices we can make.

Firstly, we may be faced with a choice between two good things. For example, if my resources of time are limited, will I do this thing or that one? A decision in this case is sometimes difficult, but not morally disturbing.

Secondly, we may be faced with the possibility of acting in what we believe is a good or bad way. This involves us in a moral choice, which is a challenge. For example, recently I was undercharged for a purchase, which I did not realise until checking the docket as I walked away. Do I keep going, or turn back and point out the mistake? I turned back, but not before I was aware of the temptation.

The third situation, in which we sometimes find ourselves, is when we are confronted by a choice between two courses of action, both of which seem to be bad. This is the classic dilemma for many loving men and women of pacifism in a time of war. However, it is not the only example. Two obvious current examples in our time concern abortion and euthanasia. These are the most difficult sorts of decisions. In these situations, I believe that when decisions are made with love, what seems to be bad is transformed into good, and what seems to be wrong is transformed into right. Any judgement is based, not on a prejudice, but on the desired outcome.

The exercise of law is to be welcomed and respected in our society, but it has no place in a community created by love. I maintain that the reliance on law is the fatal flaw in the life of the Christian Churches.

Any community ordered by love is the equivalent of the kingdom of God in the teaching of Jesus as recorded in the Gospels. It exists apart from the practice of law. It is brought into existence by the will of individuals who share common beliefs and the values that arise from them. A mutual commitment to that truth will be the creative force in a new community.

Before exploring the possibility of rebuilding the Church as a community ordered by love and not by the authority of law, it is helpful to establish in more detail the identifying marks of each. They should be regarded as indicators of the nature of the two societies, not of the individuals who may be seen as participating in them. In reality each of us is involved in both.

CHAPTER FIVE Law and Order; Love and Order

Characteristics of Each Society

Love	Law
Encourages emphasis on compassion	Encourages emphasis on justice
Encourages individual adaptability	Creates reluctance to change
Encourages self-assertiveness	Encourages aggressive attitudes
Promotes confidence	Promotes fear
Encourages honesty	Creates evasion and deceit
Promotes individual and group security	Subdues but does not resolve conflict
Promotes an egalitarian society	Creates hierarchies
Promotes trust in others	Expects obedience in others
Accepts others	Defines and labels others
Allows the present to influence the future	Establishes goals and outcomes and looks for compliance
Assesses situations before decisions	Makes judgements following precedent
Encourages a dynamic society	Produces a static society

At the outset, we must accept that both worlds are legitimate. Because of our human nature, our individuality, our instinct to survive, our freedom to choose, we recognise that we can hate and reject as easily as we can love and accept. As a consequence, we must order our human societies to control actions and practices that are agreed to be destructive of wellbeing. We must accept that this involves the development of laws and the means to enforce them.

Because each world is legitimate, each of us is able to be a willing member of both. They are, however, separate. For those whose primary commitment is to the world of love, there exists the need to learn how to relate positively to the world of law. For those whose primary commitment is to the world of law, the need is to take the contribution of the world of love seriously. This is a challenge to all of us who are inescapably involved in the one world in which we live.

CHAPTER SIX

Towards an Agreed View of Human Nature

The Christian Doctrine

A fundamental step towards an understanding and acceptance of the separation of the worlds of love and of law, while recognising that we live in both, is to establish an agreed view of human nature. The Christian Church, as it developed its doctrine, fully adopted the Old Testament belief expressed in the Genesis story of the Garden of Eden. Adam and Eve, the words in Hebrew for man and woman, were the final act of God's creation and were established in a perfect world. They were charged by God to care for and maintain it. Their disobedience, and the resultant failure to do this, was punished by expulsion from the garden and revocation of their perfect status. Only an act of God could restore it. Judaism still waits for that time. Christian doctrine asserts that it arrived when God sent Jesus, conceived by God's spirit in a woman, Mary. He was the longed-for Messiah, the one who would save humanity from that time of punishment and restore its perfect state.

Myth or Mistake

Many Christians treat these stories of creation and virgin birth as myth but accept the traditional Christian doctrine of 'original sin', which asserts that 'man is a fallen creation' and God alone can save him. If we accept that there is not, and has never been, an interventionist, supernatural God, there remains the question of whether humanity needs to be saved — what does it need to be saved from and what does it need to be saved for?

The Human Problem

Many attempts are made to deal with the problem of human behaviour in which individuals act selfishly to benefit themselves without regard for any others. This is the justification of all law. It is reasonable to suppose that the assumption that lies behind this thinking is that this is a necessity, given human nature as it is. This understanding has been reinforced in the 150 years since the publication of Charles Darwin's theory that the development of all life is through a process of evolution, governed by selection and the later development of the theory of the survival of the fittest. In this view, humans, like many other animals, are tribal creatures, creating their own territory and instinctively defending it. Acts that appear to be altruistic are, in fact in this thinking, the contribution of individuals to the tribe's survival and only secondly, therefore, to their own.

It follows that where necessity dictates, as it always will, human beings need to be saved from the consequences of their own actions. The restraint of the rule of law and the means to enforce it are designed to save people from those consequences and to ensure a more secure life.

An Alternative Christian View

The traditional Christian view is that God sent Jesus into this world, who in his divine power made the way of love real both in theory and in practice. His teaching is the theory, his life is the practice. Christian doctrine asserts that it is only by the action of God in human life that individuals are saved from destruction and for fulfilment through belief in God through Jesus.

The difficulty in accepting this lies in the experience in many races and cultures of lives lived unselfishly and loving actions observed daily without the benefit of divine intervention. The secular world in which we live offers countless examples of loving and sacrificial actions by individuals. It is instructive to consider whether, from an evolutionary perspective, rationality, intelligence, education and evolving culture are gradually releasing human beings from tribal imperatives.

Humans and Other Animals

Is it possible to find in this fact a view that while evolutionary science accurately reveals the violent propensities of human nature, it does not tell the whole story?

A start may be made by asking whether a distinction can be drawn between the human species and all others. It used to be argued that humans' big brains and ability to reason separated them from the rest. While that may be accepted as an element of differentiation, it is more and more clearly illustrated that this is only a matter of degree. Approaching the subject from another perspective, it could be argued that the ability to make the welfare of another equal to, or place it before one's own, is an essential part of all nature, and that the intellectual power of the human species has accelerated its development.

The ability to act unselfishly or sacrificially depends on the level of awareness of the individual. When we are aware of a situation, we are in a position to do something about it. Awareness of our environment is not a specifically human attribute. Some may argue that even plants exhibit a form of this when one plant placed too close to a larger one will grow away from it. However arguable that may be, it cannot be disputed that animals are aware of their environment and act in response to its influence. Humans are on the outer limit of an awareness scale. It is important to recognise, however, that there is only one scale. All living creatures, in their incredible variety, have a common heritage.

CHAPTER SIX   Towards an Agreed View of Human Nature

Evolution and Awareness

Accepting a principle of evolution in the development of species, it is not difficult to be convinced in the areas of body and mind. The body and brain of prehistoric and contemporary humans can be seen as related but different. As we now know, chimpanzees and humans have only a two per cent variation in their genes and yet they are clearly different. While the faculty of awareness is an outcome of the function of body and mind, it is a separate faculty and, therefore, part of the whole evolutionary process. This is not by its nature as evident as it is in physical evolution. It is nevertheless observable in human conduct. It is experienced and described by many as 'the life of the spirit'. The danger in using this phrase is that it may suggest there is a separate spiritual world that has an extra non-human and, therefore, religious identity. The faculty of awareness, as I describe it, relates to all life as we know it. I argue that this faculty is a third dimension in the trilogy of body, mind and spirit and that all life on every level of evolution has that potential. When I am writing about the human species, I am not writing about a divine spirit, a Holy Spirit, to which we have access, but about the human spirit, or the faculty of awareness. Human beings are creatures of body, mind and spirit.

Awareness, Religion and Law

Many thinkers have seen this faculty of awareness as the catalyst for the development of religion. Human awareness, unlike that of other species, spans past, present and future. This knowledge of the past and present, taken together with the anticipation of the future, promotes fear rather than assurance. An all-powerful God and the promise of heaven become very attractive. The development of awareness can, in the same way, be seen as the catalyst for the development of law. Both of these responses, seeking the assurance of an all-powerful God and the legal restraint of destructive forces in society, are initiated by fear, the fear of non-being and the fear of chaos.

My contention is that this two-fold response has retarded rather than encouraged the evolution of the faculty of awareness. My further contention is that human awareness is like an underground spring of water which, blocked in one place, will break through in another. There is abundant evidence of this in history. The Renaissance and the Enlightenment are two of the great examples. In countless other examples, the forces of law and religion have suffocated the human spirit. For Christians, this is the story of Jesus. He taught that perfect love dispels fear. But fear was embedded in the life of Israel, in its law and in its religion. Fear won the day and he was executed. Exactly the same patterns are visible in our world, but I believe that fear as a motivation of behaviour is slowly but surely giving way to love.

AN EVOLUTIONARY DISTINCTION

Some philosophers argue that the development of language and culture is creating an evolutionary distinction between humans and all other animals. That is an interesting and possibly correct theory. The more important issue for those who hold to the teaching of Jesus is to be reassured that the exercise of love works in the search for meaning and purpose. Whether or not a time comes when all, or even a majority, will choose to live that way is not the issue. The importance is not to be found in reaching a goal but in undertaking a journey towards it.

The witness to the truth that love dispels fear is the whole business of the Churches. The tragedy of our religious inheritance has been that, in claiming to hold that truth, the Churches, through mistaken doctrine and reliance on the processes of law, have been a barrier, not a channel, to a loving life.

CHAPTER SEVEN

Theism, Hierarchies and the Churches

I want to spell this out more clearly. The concept of theism, of a supernatural ruler of the created universe, contains within it the principle of hierarchy. Where there is a ruler there are subjects — if some are to rule as masters, others are to obey as servants. This calls for the exercise of power to control, which in turn requires the formulation of law. The Christian Church teaches that God is the supreme ruler and His subjects are many and their roles varied. The supreme ruler is infallible and unchallengeable. The roles of His subjects are determined by their response to Him. This has been described as answering a call, or accepting a vocation and the concept has not been restricted to the priesthood or ministry. One of the most potent examples of this in British history is that of the 'divine rule of kings'. This has been challenged and rejected, but lingers on in the United Kingdom where the sovereign of the state is the head of the Church and, in that role, appoints its rulers,

CHAPTER SEVEN Theism, Hierarchies and the Churches

the bishops of the Church of England. The word 'vocation' remains in a secular society, but has lost its essential meaning of being called by God.

It is a very short step in many Churches to believe that some are called to be leaders and some to be followers. The next short step is to invest leaders who are 'called by God' with God's authority. In the Roman Catholic tradition, this has been defined as the endorsement by Jesus of the apostle Peter and his successors, the popes, as God's chosen rulers of His people on earth. In each case, a line is drawn between clergy, those who are ordained and take their place in the hierarchy and are invested with the appropriate authority, and the laity who are called to obey.

While the reformations of the 16th and 17th centuries rejected much of this, emerging Calvinist and Lutheran Churches retained the division between clergy and laity and maintained it by ordination. The ordination of elders in the Calvinist tradition, who with ministers governed the Church, is an ongoing matter for debate in the Uniting Church of Australia. The independence movements of the same period, which led to the formation of the Baptist and Independent or Congregational Churches, and later movements such as Methodism, have in different degrees moved further away from the hierarchical structure of those Churches that have retained it.

The emergence in the 17th century of the Society of Friends, the Quakers as they were commonly called, has particular significance. The founder, George Fox, who died in 1691, expressed his concern about the growing rigidity of the Churches that grew out of the Reformation in the areas of doctrine, the authority of the clergy, and the form of government. He placed primary emphasis on a personal experience of the work of the Holy Spirit. This led to the rejection of priestly or ministerial vocations and the creation of the Society of Friends through which the Spirit of God worked. Anything that impeded the free movement of the Spirit was excluded and the ritual elements of worship, including the sacraments, had no part in their meeting. Any Friend who was led by the Spirit was free to speak and others were free to meditate on what they heard. The society's continuing life is witness to the element of truth contained in it.

The Uniting Church, formed from the combining of the Presbyterian and Methodist Churches with the Congregational Union in 1977, occurred on a basis that established it firmly in the two thousand-year-old life of the Christian faith, but created a form of government by councils comprised of ordained ministers and laity. Each council is responsible for the care of the Church's life in a particular sphere, from the life of a single congregation or parish, to regions, states and the Commonwealth. While this form of government aims to establish a non-hierarchical structure, it is possible to detect in its short life the emergence of practices and structures within the whole that claim greater authority and exercise greater power than can be justified. For example, there has been

CHAPTER SEVEN Theism, Hierarchies and the Churches

a movement towards the centralisation of control of the activities of its agencies. In 1977, at the time of Union, the first Synod meeting in Victoria adopted a recommendation to establish a relationship between welfare agencies, presbyteries and congregations. Individual agencies, through their councils, would have independent powers of policy development and financial administration. Congregations, or presbyteries, as sponsors, would encourage a close relationship between the institutions and the community of the Church.

Since that time the Australian Federal Government and non-government agencies have been drawn into a much closer relationship through government funding, which is dependent on acceptance of increasing control. There have been a number of situations in Victoria in which the threat of the withdrawal of registration and loss of funding has occurred. This has led to disciplinary action of the agencies and their officers by the Synod. Executive independence has been modified and a Synod position has been created through which central control is exercised. This will lead to a significantly increased bureaucracy and its outcome: the development of a hierarchy.

All this, in varying degrees, springs from the concept of theism and an adherence to the rule of law, which is brought into question by the teaching of Jesus. The Churches have developed their life from the beginning as hierarchical institutions, which, by their nature, depend on laws and their enforcement. This rule of law has led to the corruption and error which, over two thousand years, has prompted both small and large movements towards reform. The reformation of our time is to reject theism and rebuild the Church in the spirit of love.

CHAPTER EIGHT

Religion and the Churches

REFORMATION, NOT ABOLITION

Some may reject as basically impossible the claim that the new reformation of our time is to reject theism and rebuild the Church in the spirit of love. Critics argue that to reject theism is to reject religion, which is defined as an expression of belief in the divine. The proposal, however, while it involves the rejection of religion as defined, does not imply the rejection of the Churches. The two are not fundamentally linked. The Churches, as we know them, are the creation of a theistic belief. They can equally be the creation of a non-theistic belief. The foundation of the Christian Churches is the life and teaching of the man Jesus. The structures that have been built on a basic misunderstanding of that life and teaching call for reformation not abolition.

DEFENCE OF THE STATUS QUO

One of the defences Christians have made in response to attacks on their beliefs is to point to the fact that the

Christian Church is the most enduring human institution of all time. While that may be challenged, for example, by the synagogue in Judaism, it is still worth asking why it should be so. The most compelling answer may be that it is because it has, in great measure, fulfilled a human need for purpose and hope, for loving and being loved. We should ask why, in our time, the fastest growing Christian communities are those whose teachings are presented in an authoritative form that elicits from their members an enthusiastic response. When the world feels unsafe and when leaders conduct successful election campaigns largely based on insecurity and fear, many look for the haven of an authoritarian faith.

One of the marks of these fast-growing Christian Churches is the emotional response of individuals to the promise of security and the experience of inclusion in a loving and caring community. This, in itself, is not a matter for criticism. On another level, however, it is a matter for concern. Fear cannot be truly dispelled by any form of authoritarian teaching. Fear belongs to the world of law and the forces that come from outside us. The free response to love in life comes from within us.

Theistic Christianity teaches that the love of God, offered to us, makes this possible. That conviction has generated a power of love that has created and sustained families, changed societies, abolished cruel laws and maintained the life of the Christian Church through two thousand years. In that case, why challenge it?

CHAPTER EIGHT   Religion and the Churches

Meeting the Challenge

The answers may be manifold, but three reasons are sufficient.

Firstly, it is based on a false assumption about the existence of God, which should no longer be regarded as fact but as myth, defined as an attempt to understand the events of life that are beyond human comprehension. As knowledge advances, there are fewer mysteries. There is, however, no mystery about the teaching of Jesus, which is self-authenticating, and where its acceptance depends on an inward response of individuals and communities, not an imposed one.

Secondly, the concept of theism inevitably leads to the establishment of hierarchies and to the formulation of law. The exercise of law leads to the formation of societies that cannot escape corruption and subsequent ongoing legal refinement. For example, by the first century of the Christian era, there was a huge body of law in Judaism governing the observance of the sabbath day, which grew out of one of the Ten Commandments delivered by Moses.

Thirdly, to reject theism is not to deny the possibility of experiencing a power that transcends our individuality. One of the less obvious but most potent destructive forces in theistic Christianity is to teach that only a belief in God makes that possible. Politically, there is a great deal of emphasis on 'people power' in our time. It is one of the signs of the recovery of the sense of community that the Churches have experienced in the past. As individuals, we are aware that being committed to an idea or a cause or a relationship releases strengths and abilities that we possess. When a commitment is shared with others, the whole becomes greater than the sum of the parts and an even greater force is released. To attribute this to a supernatural force allows us to deny to others the fullness of our love. It makes a mockery of the life of Jesus while we indulge in the comfort of worship. This love is an expression of our humanity, not of any access to divinity. Theism degrades the nature of our humanity when our prayers ask for outcomes that should be our business.

Reformation and the Rule of Law

In moving towards the reformation of a theistically based Christian Church and the emergence of a non-theistically based one, we must recognise that the exercise of law is a tool that may be used either to benefit or to exploit. Wise and benevolent laws encourage outcomes of security and justice, but foolish and self-interested laws lead to outcomes of chaos and persecution. However, it needs to be understood that all law, whether benevolent or self-interested, is based on the need to control through imposed restraints. Even benevolent law uses fear to promote its objective. For individuals or societies to be ruled by fear is to diminish life.

On the other hand, we also know that while law puts restraints on us, our experience of loving and being loved leads to a sense of freedom. For our mistakes there is understanding, and for our guilt there is forgiveness. Some will choose, as a priority, to commit themselves to creating and building caring and loving communities. Others in positions of authority in our societies may, at worst, use law to exploit others, but, at best, may commit themselves to the reduction of forces that lead to ever-more repressive law.

The teaching of Jesus indicates that communities that are created and maintained by the spirit of love, while never large, may have a large effect on societies created and maintained by the rule of law.

Many of us have individually tried to maintain our commitment to a life ordered by love. Some have remained loyal to their Churches, while others have looked to other beliefs. Large numbers have opted for material security. Our children have not found intellectual or emotional fulfilment in the Churches they have known.

It would not be wise to underrate the opposition to the ideas that have been expressed here. The Churches, as they are, see themselves as the custodians of truth. The views I have expressed reject the doctrine of theism. They are not an attack on the teaching and life of Jesus. Communities that still want to identify with the past life of the Church but rejecting theism will be challenged as heretical. The only answer to that is in the words of Jesus: 'You will recognise them by their fruits.'

PART TWO

CHAPTER NINE

Examining the Bible

I have indicated that it is not my intention to discuss the details of the outcomes of biblical scholarship. There are many books readily available in these areas for those who are interested in both conservative and radical scholarship. I am writing from what has been distilled through my experience, and the opinions I have expressed need to be justified. My concern here is with the interpretation of the teaching of Jesus as it is recorded in the Gospels. Before we are able to focus on that, we must briefly consider the Bible as a whole.

THE BIBLE IS THE CREATION OF THE CHURCH

The Bible is a compilation, determined by the early Church, of writings related to the long history of Israel and the Jewish people: a record of the life and teaching of Jesus in the Gospels; an account of events following his death; Paul's letters to the young Churches he founded; and some other letters and writings in the second half of the first century AD.

The Bible may be divided into three elements that are not equally important to Christian understanding. The Old Testament may be regarded as the story of the preparation for the events of the New; thus, a line is drawn between the Old and New Testaments. Within the New Testament, however, another distinction must be drawn between the Gospels and the remainder. The former constitutes the record of the life and teaching of Jesus, the latter the record of the events following his death and resurrection. First importance must be given to the Gospels — anything written before, or after them, however important it may be, must be regarded as secondary.

THE GOSPELS

Mark's story, the earliest of the four Gospels, was written at least thirty years after the death of Jesus; the other three were written over the next fifty years. Although Matthew, Mark and Luke have been regarded as eye-witnesses, Mark and Luke were not. John, who wrote at the end of the first century, was probably not an apostle.

The Gospel authors were creatures of their own age. They were Jews or greatly influenced by Judaism and the beliefs of their time. Their world encouraged them to believe in the promise of someone, a Messiah, who would save them. They believed that they were a people chosen by God for this purpose. Their God was the only God. He was the creator and ruler of the universe and He would, as

He had done before, intervene in their world. They were ready for a saviour.

They also shared a common world view. They believed that both God and Satan had dwelling places beyond their world. They thought the world was flat. One idea was that it was covered by a dome that held back the waters in which it was suspended. The flood, for example, according to one account, occurred when the windows of heaven opened. There were many mysteries in their life, but this one was explained by understanding that cataclysmic event as revealing God's displeasure at man's evil. His decision was to drown all except Noah, a good man, his family and representatives of the animal creation so that He could start over again.

There were many other mysteries created by the limited knowledge of the Gospel writers. Nevertheless, overcoming all mysteries and doubts was the promise of God's care for them. The Law, given by God to Moses, and developed and reinforced over their whole history, was the vehicle of their salvation. The Temple, with the ritual practice of animal sacrifice at its heart, ensured the continuing favour of their God in spite of individual and national sin. While these were beliefs held in common, the Gospel writers were additionally influenced by their own personal circumstances.

MATTHEW

Matthew's account includes many references to the Old Testament that do not appear in other accounts. They sometimes appear as a sort of additional note to stories that are repeated in the other Gospels and attributed to Jesus. They often introduce references to Jewish Law and the punishment of wrongdoers. His Gospel seems to be particularly directed to and designed to engage the interest of a Jewish audience. The growth of the early Church was often based on synagogues established by dispersed Jewish communities. The date usually assigned to its origin is between 80 and 90 AD.

MARK

Mark's account, the earliest of the four, is the simplest and shortest. According to an early tradition, Mark was a young man who happened to witness the arrest of Jesus in the Garden of Gethsemane. He later had some connection with Paul, but more significantly was a companion of Peter. The same tradition identified his account as he learned it from Peter. His is the earliest of the accounts as we have them and was written about the year 65 AD.

LUKE

Luke, a later Gentile convert, had access to Mark's account and to earlier, but now lost, records. He describes in a sort of explanatory note at the beginning of his Gospel that he 'decided to write a connected narrative ... so as to give ...

authentic knowledge'. The assumption that lies behind this is that, by his time, non-authentic or partial accounts were circulating orally or in writing. The probable date of his account is around 75–80 AD.

John

John's Gospel is separated from the so-called synoptic accounts. It was written in the last decade of the first century, and for that and other reasons it is assumed by many commentators to be the work not of John, one of the first twelve disciples, but of someone influenced by John, who lived as an old man in Ephesus. It is obviously written at a time when Greek thought and language had exerted a greater influence in the communities where the story of the Gospel was being told. He records some of the same events in Jesus' life, but in a way that reveals a great deal of reflection on them. He writes of the close identification of Jesus with the Father in a way that admits no separation. He describes the experience of entering the kingdom of God as a present and eternal spiritual possibility. The most striking difference from the first three Gospels is that, whereas they record the moral teaching of Jesus, the only reference in John is to his directive: 'Love one another, as I have loved you.' Because of this difference, John's account must be considered separately.

The Fundamental Elements

There have been many attempts to extract the authentic

teaching and accurate accounts of Jesus' life from the available records. This is not only difficult, but in the long run not wholly possible. What we have in the four Gospels has to be the most reliable, not only because they appeared in the first century, but because they have been adopted by those in the best position to judge at the time. This does not present any difficulty for those who believe that every word of the Gospels is fundamentally true as the God-inspired writing of the authors. This belief, however, can be challenged on many grounds. Biblical criticism, an academic discipline, has many examples of both words and actions in the four accounts to support this conviction. The authors, both in a minor and major way, have varied the words and actions of Jesus. They drew on earlier records, which are now lost. They used both the same sources and some that are unique to each.

These comparatively superficial observations are enough to illustrate that within the four accounts, as we have them, there is abundant evidence of the development over the following seventy years of the records of the events occurring around 30 AD. However, it is still possible to detect the fundamental elements of Jesus' life and teaching that are at the core of every account.

CHAPTER TEN

The Fundamental Teaching

INTRODUCTION

In retrospect, it is no surprise to me that in my ministry I have not been particularly troubled by its theistic content. However, some things I have avoided. I have never been comfortable with the form of prayer called intercession, especially when I was asked to pray for specific people or occasions. Prayers of preparation, of confession and of thanksgiving, and moments of meditation, did not trouble me at all. While I appreciated the loving concern of those who asked for, or expected, specific prayers for specific people, I could not see the justification for it. Surely, God did not have to be told about it, and if His response was conditional on people making a request, it seemed to be not only unloving but unjust. I did not need to avoid references to hell as a future place for punishment — those who heard me preach did not believe in it either.

However, in the twenty-two years since I retired, I have become increasingly reluctant to accede to requests to conduct services and have not conducted regular ones for a long time, but, when asked, I have very rarely refused the request to celebrate weddings or funerals. I inherited a tradition from my Presbyterian background that offered guidance in forms of worship. However, a minister — apart from the celebration of the sacraments — was free to determine its content. In the very personal occasions of funerals and weddings, I have fashioned the service following the beliefs of the people involved.

On one occasion, after a very large and public funeral, one friend thanked me saying that he greatly appreciated it, but added that he didn't notice 'much reference to "the Big G" in it'. I valued his response, but was aware that there would have been some present on that occasion who did not share his reaction.

That awareness is reinforced by the increasing tendency in the Uniting Church to issue directives to ministers in this and other matters. Law and regulation are creeping into the message of love and freedom. I understand but do not accept the view that we need to use law in the life of a community based on the teaching of Jesus.

Throughout this chapter, I am referring to the teaching in its original setting. In the next, I will recast it in a setting adjusted to an understanding of our world today.

THE GOSPEL SOURCES

The first written record in our possession dates from 65–75 AD, more than thirty years after Jesus' death, which prompts the question as to whether this account stems from oral sources only, or from other documents now lost. Mark's account was used by Luke and Matthew during the next thirty years and John probably had access to all three at the end of the century. Luke and Matthew had access to other sources that were not part of Mark's earlier account and were not common to each other. We are, therefore, able to discern the existence but not the detail of additional sources. It is also reasonable to assume that Mark's account was based on more than oral tradition thirty years after the event. This source is thought to be a collection of the sayings of Jesus. Analysis of the texts of the Gospels allows us to understand not only why some parables and sayings appear only once, but also the presence of discrepancies of occasion and context. In looking for the fundamentals of the teaching, it is reasonable to apply the principle that one part of the record that differs from the rest must be evaluated by reference to the whole.

Background

Jesus was born in Bethlehem and emerged as a teacher at about the age of thirty. He quickly attracted the attention of the people about him. From the first of these, he asked twelve to join him as he took his message to his nation, Israel. He believed he had a universal message for the world, but knew that he had to locate his teaching in his own time and space. His was a nation that believed itself to be a people with a unique destiny. Israel existed to be the vehicle of the truth about life, which was being progressively revealed through its history. This truth was enshrined in laws they believed had been divinely revealed. A system of law had been developed over many generations and its custodians had developed their authority to teach and administer it. They are identified in the story as lawyers, scribes and Pharisees. In Jesus' time, laws with a divine authority touched every aspect of daily life in Israel. Jesus believed that the people's lives had been corrupted by the misuse of both the Law and the power exercised by those who administered it. This was a central theme of his message. The story, in Matthew and Luke, known as the Temptations, was an individual solitary experience of Jesus at the beginning of his mission. He related it to those he had asked to join him before they set out with him.

THE TEMPTATIONS OF JESUS

One temptation was to capitalise on the first enthusiastic response to his presence. Under the oppression of Roman occupation and corrupt law, the people were ready for the promise of better things and a more hopeful future. Rome extracted taxes from all the territories they occupied and tax collectors, many of whom were local Jews, extracted more. The result was economic hardship and poverty. A temptation was to exploit this situation and use the promise of material recovery to gain acceptance.

Another was to exploit the people's belief in the existence of devils, supernatural evil beings who created physical and mental havoc in their lives. At the same time, they believed in a God who would intervene to save them, and this predisposed them to the idea of supernatural intervention. It would have been tempting to exploit this potent belief.

Finally, there was the temptation to compromise. What Jesus was intending to teach was sure to arouse great hostility: from the country's leaders, from the occupying power of Rome; from those who benefitted from the occupation; and from all who would be disturbed by his radical message. Would it be better to compromise with those who controlled their society and hope to change it without antagonising them?

Jesus' Response

His message was simple and clear, it was profound and revolutionary, and it was directed specifically to individuals. Power can be used to control by imposing restrictions and has a legitimate place in any nation or society. It is, however, dangerous in the wrong hands and a fertile ground for corruption. Power can also be used to set others free. The nature of that type of power is love. This is not corruptible. It is a basic truth about life. The power of law can only restrict life. The power of love can only create abundant, fulfilled life. This having been made clear to his disciples, Jesus set out on his mission to teach and to heal, to set the people free. 'You will know the truth,' he said, 'and the truth will make you free.'

THE KINGDOM OF GOD

This teaching was principally conveyed through the central idea of 'the kingdom of God'. This use of the concept of a kingdom of God would have immediately resonated with his audience. Israel saw itself as a nation and a kingdom. This was both an ideal and a political reality. It was, for them, not just another kingdom, but one chosen by God and maintained through centuries as the instrument of His purpose for His creation. There were two distinct views on the nature of the kingship. One was of the warrior king. Given their history of invasion by neighbouring powers, this is not surprising. This expression of kingship, however, was not the only one. From the beginning of the monarchy, the role of the king was to be a servant of his people. Being a victorious warrior was seen as a service to them, but one war led to another, often with disastrous results.

There was another powerful influence exerted through the nation's life. Kings were continually challenged by prophets. A prophet was recognised by both king and people as one inspired by the spirit of God to reveal His ongoing will for them. This led to many confrontations between kings and prophets. One of the greatest prophets was Isaiah, who, observing the limited results of war, saw another way.

A servant king could also promote reconciliation and peace and this, in fact, was seen as a truer expression of God's will for His people. Both these ideas were present in the national consciousness.

CHAPTER TEN The Fundamental Teaching

The concept of the kingdom is described in Mark and Luke as the 'kingdom of God', in Matthew as the 'kingdom of heaven'. In John it is only used once, but the same reality is conveyed in the concept of eternal life. The variation is significant. Mark and Luke's description is understood as life in which God is known, accepted and lived in accordance with His will. There is a similar understanding in John's use of the concept of eternal life. There it can be understood as a quality of life determined by a belief in Jesus as God's son and dependent on His spirit. Matthew uses the phrase 'kingdom of heaven', which involves the idea of a location separate from the earth.

THE PARABLES

Jesus' teaching was partly expressed in parables. These are simple stories with a concealed meaning. The parable of the sower appears early in the first three Gospels and is distinguished by Jesus' comment that if the disciples understood this one, they would understand them all. The story describes a farmer spreading seed in soil that varied from the least to the most productive. Much of the seed was wasted, but where it fell on the most fertile ground each resulting plant flourished and a great harvest resulted. This, at the beginning, indicated a subsequently recurrent theme that Jesus was not launching a mass movement which would expel the occupying forces and abolish the system of law that dominated their life. On the contrary, he was establishing a community that would be essentially small. The power of this community would be like a light shining in darkness; salt in a meal; yeast in a baker's flour; a tiny seed of mustard which could grow into a great tree; a single but immensely valuable pearl; a treasure which, buried out of sight, would still exert great influence; a net lowered into the sea gathering a great catch of fish. The power of this community would be directed not to the control of the nation and its people, but to setting them free to experience an abundant, fulfilled life.

His disciples frequently questioned him about the meanings of his parables and his replies are part of the record. When they asked why he used this device in the story of the sower, his answer was that it allowed his teaching to be understood by those who would welcome it, but would obscure it from those who would not. Only Mark adds to this explanation that this was in case those who would not understand might do so and 'turn to God and be forgiven'. This is a reference to the Old Testament as a means of adding authority to the story. It is related to the recorded call by God to the prophet Isaiah and the instruction to: 'Make the heart of this people fat, and their ears heavy ... lest they hear with their ears, and understand with their hearts, and turn and be healed.' This is almost certainly a later scribe's addition to Mark's text — a common practice. It is taken out of context from Isaiah, does not appear in the other records of the story, and is inconsistent with the intention of Jesus. The more likely explanation is that this use of the parable was designed to

CHAPTER TEN   The Fundamental Teaching

minimise the hostility that was growing around Jesus. His later decision to retreat to the north, when he was facing growing opposition from the authorities in the south, is consistent with this view. This example illustrates the difficulty of distinguishing the actual words of Jesus from editorial additions. One method of solving the problem is by comparing accounts and adopting the more common one, or that which is more consistent with the rest of the record.

Thus far, the form of the kingdom is indicated. It is to be a community created by those who live their lives to benefit others. It is dynamic and continually developing, as those who, inspired by Jesus, adopt it and set out on a journey together. The community itself is to be a continuing demonstration of its beliefs.

Necessary Attributes for Discipleship

Faith and trust are the necessary attributes in taking the first step on this journey. The first twelve disciples would have been, each in his own way, ready to take that step. Although the accounts are almost entirely devoid of any detail about their background, in general terms we know that they lived in some sort of expectation of the appearance of a person who was promised in their scriptures as the Messiah. It was an act of faith for them to accede to his invitation, 'Follow me.' This act of faith is reinforced by Jesus' frequently recorded words to those who sought his help: 'Your faith has saved you'; 'Never have I seen such faith'; 'O you of little faith, how I grieve for you.' It is expressed in his comment that childlike acceptance is the way into the life of this community, of identifying with the kingdom of God.

There is a strong emphasis in the teaching on commitment. This is established in the initial decision of the first twelve disciples to immediately go with him, and reinforced by many comments throughout the accounts like: 'No-one who sets his hand to the plough and then keeps looking back is fit for the kingdom of God.' This would have been a strong challenge and it created an anxiety that is occasionally expressed. This feeling of insecurity was met by the assurance that, individually and together, their needs would be met. The primary thing was to live fully in the present and not devalue its importance by being anxious about the future.

Authority and the Role of Law

A great deal of the teaching arose out of the challenges it provoked from the custodians of the Law, the lawyers and Pharisees. From the beginning, they questioned Jesus' authority to act and teach as he did. The observance of the sabbath day was central to the dispute. The Law governing this practice had been developed in great detail and was one of the easiest for the leaders to use to maintain their position. When Jesus broke one of these laws and was challenged, his reply was, 'Man was not made for the sabbath but the sabbath for man.' His words were

CHAPTER TEN The Fundamental Teaching

encouraging listeners to question the Law. Therefore, Jesus was seen as a dangerous radical whose teaching would undermine the basis of the society that was sanctioned by God, and who was disputing the authority of the leaders. There are some important things to note. Jesus, without exception, avoided any direct answer to a challenge to his authority. Those who were impressed by his actions or his words are reported as being amazed by the authority they carried. They compared this with the instruction they received from the Pharisees. His was self-authenticating — theirs was dependent on a body of sanctioned law.

Jesus did, however, recognise the necessity of law as an instrument to regulate society. The often-quoted example of this is his reply to the lawyers who tried to trap him by a question about Roman taxation, a hotly debated issue of the day. Asking to see a coin that carried an image of the emperor, he held it out and said, 'Pay Caesar what is due to Caesar, and pay God what is due to God.'

More significantly, on one occasion when he was asked by a lawyer which was the primary commandment, Jesus replied that it was to love God and your neighbour as yourself. When his questioner agreed, Jesus assured the lawyer that he was not far from the kingdom of God. Jesus taught that his message was not a denial of the Law but its fulfilment. It was not the fact of Law, but the way it was practised by the rulers that he totally rejected. Law embodied the concept of control and was easily corrupted. His message was about freedom.

THE NATURE OF LAW AND THE NATURE OF LOVE

A great deal of the criticism of the leaders arose from their dependence on outward conformity to the Law, which involved every aspect of human behaviour and the hypocrisy that it generated. Some of the most graphic illustrations Jesus used came from the laws governing the nature, preparation and eating of food. It was not what went into the mouth but what came out of it that mattered. Expressed in a different way, he taught that only a good tree produced good fruit. Living by Law, which demanded outward conformity without regard to its true purpose — to lead people to live good lives — resulted in hypocrisy and exploitation.

One of the major outcomes of this rule of Law was to establish the attitude that some members of society were ordained by God to rule and others to obey. There were clear distinctions between masters and servants. Jesus taught that in the kingdom of God this distinction was invalid. Masters were not greater than servants, and servants not greater than masters. Even at the end of the disciples' association with Jesus, some of them still hadn't got the message. When Jesus, before his last meal with them, took the role of a servant who customarily washed guests' feet as they arrived from the street, Peter refused him. Jesus' response was to say to him that if he could not accept what he had done, then he did not understand the heart of his life and teaching. Leaders were servants and had to be seen as servants. Unlike the Pharisees who dressed to indicate their rank and made their good works obvious, the disciples were to ensure that their behaviour was never a matter for display. They were not to act in order to impress.

FORGIVENESS

Jesus was spelling out an ideal. His followers, right to the end and beyond it, fell short. It is not surprising that forgiveness was a basic ingredient of his message. Asked how often one must forgive a brother — the suggested number of times being seven — Jesus' reply was that it must be seventy times seven: in other words, not exactly 490 times, but always. The only exception to this was an offence against the Holy Spirit. These words, 'Holy Spirit', probably not original ones of Jesus, are a later doctrinal description and are not used in any other context of his teaching. If we describe the unforgivable offence as one against the spirit, it clearly does not make sense. The spirit in Jesus' terms is the activity of love; and disciples then, as now, who have offended against it have been forgiven.

In his healing acts, Jesus repeatedly linked illness and derangement with sin by declaring, 'Your sins are forgiven.' While this reflected the common belief that illness was God's punishment for sin, he was again challenging their law which taught that only God could forgive sin.

JUDGEMENT AND PUNISHMENT

The administration of law leads to the judgement and punishment of those who break it. Where there is no law, there is no judgement. Jesus' words, 'Do not judge' and 'I have not come to judge the world but save it', are consistent with his teaching about law in the kingdom of God. To love God and your neighbour as yourself cannot be motivated or ordered by law.

It is surprising, then, to read in the records of Matthew and Luke of some parables told in the days shortly before his arrest. At the end of these stories, words suggesting that God will punish those who reject Him are attributed to Jesus. These embellishments can be seen as additions to the parables. The stories are all part of the record of encounters and disputes with the Pharisees and lawyers who were at this time planning his death. They apply to that situation but are manipulated to reflect a view that is inconsistent with the teaching.

John's account approaches the whole question about judgement through the concept of light and darkness. In Jesus, the light of God has entered the world. This reveals truth and illuminates it. It also reveals the existence of darkness. People have a choice between coming to the light and remaining in the dark. Their choice determines their life. Those who live in the light enter into eternal life. It is implied that living in darkness carries its own penalty. There is no imposed judgement.

IMPEDIMENTS TO DISCIPLESHIP

Throughout the teaching, there are references to impediments to entry into this new life. Reliance on the establishment and practice of law is the greatest. Another is reliance on material security — it is hard for a rich man to enter the kingdom: 'You cannot serve God and Mammon.' Any competing interests, like claims of family, or lack of single-mindedness, persistence or self-discipline, are impediments.

Sayings of Jesus

A collection of Jesus' remembered sayings is to be found in the accounts of Matthew and Luke. In Matthew's, this is known as 'The Sermon on the Mount', which is recorded in chapters 5–7. Despite the fact that it is possible to detect a few things that are embellishments influenced by contemporary thought, this passage is a remarkable summary of the teaching and an illustration of Jesus' life. He lived what he taught.

The Fourth Gospel

As has been mentioned previously, John's Gospel takes us into another sphere. One of the major differences is the almost total omission of the moral teaching. This may well be because the author, writing at the close of the first century, was well aware of the existing three accounts and saw no need to repeat them. This, however, is not the critical difference. Morality and moral codes have either an informal social basis or a formal legal one. The one basis for behaviour in the teaching of Jesus is that we should love our neighbour. This is the dynamic of the life that

Jesus taught and lived. At its heart his teaching provides no basis for the codification of behaviour.

It was John's intention to record what he believed was the essential meaning of the life of Jesus. He asserted that Christ's life was a manifestation of the presence and power of God in creation from the beginning. Eternity was the past, the present and the future.

John was not, therefore, primarily concerned with historical accuracy. He placed elements of the common story at different times and in different settings. A primary example of this is the positioning of the occasion on which Jesus denounced those who were using the Temple as a source of profit for themselves — of turning the house of God into a 'den of thieves' — at the beginning of his mission, not at the end where the other accounts record it. He includes some of the miracles but describes them as 'miracles and signs'. John makes no reference to the familiar birth stories; places the Temple incident to indicate that it was a sign of the cleansing of the nation's life; and records the story of the changing of water into wine at a marriage feast as the first sign that this was not just a cleansing, but an enriching of life. One of the few parables unique to this account is that of the good shepherd who will lay down his life for his sheep. This introduces all the events that took place at the end of Jesus' life.

CHAPTER TEN The Fundamental Teaching

THE SON AND THE FATHER

A continual emphasis in John is the identification of God the Father with Jesus the Son. Jesus is recorded as saying many times, 'He who has seen me has seen God,' or very similar statements. It is as though the idea of God becoming man, which is at the heart of traditional Christian teaching, can be as easily stated as man becoming God. This concept is extended to establish that knowledge and acceptance of the man Jesus is to obtain eternal life. For John, as for the other three authors, this is a gift available in the present life of individuals.

LIFE AFTER DEATH

John's concept seems to extend more clearly the experience for individuals beyond their mortal death. This, at first sight, seems to be the message in what are known as 'The Farewell Discourses of Jesus' contained in chapters 13–17 of John's Gospel. These, as reported by John, were addressed to the eleven disciples after Judas had betrayed him and left them during their last meal together. It is from this record that a central part of the Christian funeral ritual is drawn in which Jesus' words are used: 'There are many dwelling places in my Father's house ... I am going there on purpose to prepare a place for you. And if I go and prepare a place for you, I will come again and receive you to myself, so that where I am you may be also.'

John's account suggests a different interpretation of these last words of Jesus. The central element of this record is the constantly repeated theme of the love that has been the motivation of every aspect of their life with him to this point, and the injunction to go on loving in the future as he has loved them. This will be a future without him, but it is not the tragedy that they perceive it to be — it is the necessary condition for the future. It is for their good that he is leaving them because, when he goes, his mission will be fulfilled through them. He tells them not to be afraid because, although he is going away, he will be coming back and will be with them in Spirit. This will be in their shared life, informed by the love and truth that is their present and will be their future experience. They will no longer think of him as Master and Lord and themselves as servants, but as friends together. The way for them to understand this is to think of the life of a vine. They are to think of him as the real vine and of God as the gardener — the life-force of the universe — who will ensure its health. In these terms, they are to think of themselves as branches, part of the vine, and being united with it in bearing a great crop of fruit. In this way, they will do greater things than he has done with them in the past.

THE WAY FORWARD

In his final prayer with his disciples and for them, Jesus thinks of them still in the world and does not pray that they should be taken out of it. He prays not only for them but for all who will share their new life in the Spirit. He prays that they may be where he is, that they may be with

CHAPTER TEN The Fundamental Teaching

him, and that he may be with them. This is where love will be made real in the life of the world they know.

Summary

In summary, at the centre of Jesus' teaching is the invitation to live a life empowered by the love of God with all one's being, and to reflect that devotion through love of those with whom we share our life. This is an invitation, not a command. It is a life lived by an inner conviction, not by an imposed authority. It is completely different from life in a society that is ordered by law. It is like new clothes, not patches on old ones, or like the use of new wineskins to contain new wine.

It is life in a community created and sustained by love. It will be a community within the wider society that is maintained by law. Individuals within its fellowship will continue to acknowledge and accept the wider society governed by law, but in clear separation from it. The points at which these will intersect will be those at which the community of love is able to influence the society of law. The influence will be like light seen from a hill; salt to flavour food; leaven to enable flour to lighten a loaf of bread; a tiny seed that can grow into a large tree; a single pearl of great price; a hidden treasure; a fishing net thrown into the sea.

The old world is the way of law for all — the new is the way of love for all. The new world will experience love made real. The old world will see it.

CHAPTER ELEVEN

Adjusting the Gospel Setting

A belief in one God whose dwelling is in heaven, but whose influence is exercised throughout His creation, provides the overall setting of the Gospel story. This doctrine is described as theism. It finds expression in the concept of a Law of God originating in Moses, and is developed in the life of His chosen people Israel; in a Messiah, a divine person sent by God to complete His purpose for them; in God's supernatural intervention throughout their history; and a belief in a final trial and judgement of each individual.

This belief, though not shared by the larger world of the time, was the basic assumption of the world into which Jesus was born. Though he expressed his teaching in that context, it must be stressed that it is totally concerned with human life. The central message of his teaching is about universal love, but cast in specific terms about human relationships. While he used the theistic expressions of his time, the teaching stands alone in its own right. It reveals no idea of formulated doctrine and only the faintest outline of a possible Church — in his recorded words at the last meal with his disciples, 'Do this to remember me.'

The young Church in the first century of the Christian Era lived in the environment of the Jewish Law, which was God's Law. It was believed to be given initially in the Ten Commandments delivered to Moses on Mount Sinai as he led Israel out of slavery towards a promised land. This God was the only God, the creator and supreme ruler of the world and the God who chose Israel to fulfil His purpose for His creation. The authority for Christians, as for Israel, is traced back to a supernatural God who is supreme.

Examining the Gospels reveals that, while inspired by the life and teaching of Jesus, they are not divinely dictated but are the record of a human response to his life. In the same way in which Jesus challenged the fundamental teaching of the religious leaders of his day, his life and teaching challenge the concept of theism in the following ways.

JESUS AVOIDED TITLES FOR HIMSELF THAT IMPLIED A DIVINE IDENTITY

He chose for himself the descriptive title 'Son of Man', in contrast to that which others bestowed on him, such as: 'Son of God', 'The Christ', 'The Messiah'. 'Son of Man' derives from the Old Testament and was therefore familiar to his Jewish audience. It implies that he thought of himself as a fully human being — a son of man. The other titles imply his supernatural origin and identity. These he avoided.

He Did Not Claim any Divine Authority

While the Jewish leaders claimed for themselves the authority of God through the Law, Jesus consistently refused to respond to the frequent challenges to his authority. He lived and spoke as a man. His life and teaching spoke for itself. His message was self-authenticating.

God Became Man? Or Man Became God?

John's Gospel identifies God and Jesus as one. Unlike the other three, his record reports many instances when Jesus says words like, 'He who has seen me has seen the Father.' Theistically, this is accepted that in Jesus 'God became man.' It may more truly be interpreted that in Jesus' teaching what was thought of as a supernatural God was human love in man.

Examining the Miracles

The Gospels contain many references to miracles, which are presented as evidence of Jesus' supernatural origin and power. In many accounts, the possibility that the stories may stem from the seed of an observed event, and not be a total invention, must be considered.

Miracles have been reported in our own time. When the German forces were advancing on the retreating Allies at Dunkirk in the Second World War, there seemed no chance

CHAPTER ELEVEN   Adjusting the Gospel Setting

of a large-scale evacuation from the beaches of France to the safety of England. Few large ships were available and the weather was very stormy and forecast to worsen. Then, unexpectedly, a great calm settled on the English Channel. A multitude of little boats set out from and returned to English ports, bringing thousands of soldiers back to safety. All over the Allied world, Church services were held to give thanks to God for this deliverance. It was, people said, a miracle. Many, probably a majority, would explain this Second World War experience as an error in forecasting linked to a weather change, which allowed an outcome that turned a potential disaster into a successful rescue.

We are also familiar with the ministries of 'faith healers'; many claim to have been miraculously cured by participating in healing services. There seems no doubt that some claims to be healed are valid. How they occur is open to interpretation in the light of other facts. Medical assessments of the outcomes of healing by faith sometimes explain the facts, not by miraculous intervention, but as spontaneous remissions of disease. In other cases, the disorders are described as hysterical — conditions involving blindness, deafness, dumbness and paralysis that have their origin in psychological, not physical, conditions. In neither of these situations can the 'healing' be attributed to some supernatural intervention but are understandable in natural terms.

Without embarking on a process of examining the Gospel stories one by one through the whole record, we can broadly consider the alternatives. The environment in which these events occurred encouraged the expectation of the miraculous. There are many events in the history of the Jewish people recorded in the Old Testament that were attributed to God's intervention. One of the better known is the parting of the waters of the Red Sea, which enabled Moses and his followers to escape the pursuing Egyptians.

In a world of restricted knowledge of the causal connection between events, it was easy to attribute divine intervention to them when no other cause could be perceived. A number of the healing stories recounted as miracles fall into the category of what would now be seen as the cure of hysterical illnesses, those that have a physical manifestation but a psychological origin. The accounts of apparently dead people being brought back to life can be seen as recovery from a deep coma. It is reasonable to understand details in the Gospel, which seem to preclude that explanation, as due to the gradual embroidering of an original natural event for at least three reasons. One is the thirty to seventy years elapsing between the time of its happening and the final recording of it in a superstitious age. Another is to emphasise the supernatural element as proof of the divine power of Jesus. This leads to more prosaic explanations, which could be seen as political reasons, including the bolstering of the authority of the custodians of the newly emerging Church in the latter third of the first century. Yet another is the development of doctrine in the emerging institution, which was designed

CHAPTER ELEVEN Adjusting the Gospel Setting

to support the structure as the repository of the truth that it validated.

The doctrine of the Virgin Birth of Jesus is a sufficient example. The concept of a virgin birth was present in other cultures of the time. For the young Church, it was an ideal vehicle to convey the perceived idea that Jesus was both divine and human, conceived by God and born of woman. The birth stories do not appear in the first account, written in about 65 AD, or in the last, which appeared at the end of the first century.

THE IDEA ABOUT A RETURN OF JESUS

Another way in which the teaching of Jesus was misunderstood and distorted was in the development of the idea of his return after his death to complete his mission, which would be a time of reckoning and judgement and occur in the foreseeable future. However, his teaching was that the kingdom of God was a present reality for those who adopted it. The early announcement, 'The time has come: the kingdom of God is upon you'; and the later words — 'There are some standing here who will see the kingdom of God come with power'; 'There are some here who will not taste death before they have seen the Son of Man coming in his kingdom'; 'Be sure the kingdom of God has already come upon you'; and 'The kingdom of God is within you' — all support this understanding.

This idea became widespread and was linked to that of the reward of believers and the judgement and punishment of the rest. It is this situation that almost certainly led to the insertion of words attributed to Jesus in the later records of Luke and Matthew that are not consistent with the rest of his teaching.

As time passed, and this speculation was shown to be false, it was interpreted as a mistake in timing and not as a crucial error in understanding the teaching. It was, of course, wrong on both counts. The belief in a 'second coming' has survived to our own time, but it is still wrong. It now seems to be attached to the more fundamentalist beliefs, but is still embedded in doctrine. Many Christians in the mainstream of belief are still asked to subscribe to the creedal statement that Jesus will come 'to judge the living and the dead'.

SUMMARY

When the theistic setting is removed, we are led to abandon the idea of the Bible as a divinely inspired, authoritative and infallible record of God's revelation. We are then able to see it as a record of a human response to life as it has been experienced in one nation and people, and in the emergence of a man whose teaching revealed a universal understanding of the nature of human life that leads to fulfilment, not in a future life but in this present one.

CHAPTER TWELVE

The Teaching of Jesus as a Way of Life for Today

Introduction

I have maintained in Chapter Nine, titled 'Examining the Bible', that while the Bible is comprised of different elements, they are not equally important as sources to establish the teaching of Jesus and the events of his life. In this, primacy must be given to the Gospels, but I do not claim that the other parts of the Bible are irrelevant.

The Old Testament, the history of Israel, is important as the heritage of Jesus and of the nation into which he was born. The Christian Church has understood it as the story of God's preparation for the birth of the Messiah, Jesus.

The Acts of the Apostles, written by Luke, take the story from the first days after the resurrection of Jesus to the account of Paul's last journey, which took him to Rome.

The greater part of the rest comprises letters Paul wrote to young Christian communities that he had founded. They are largely prompted by reports of disputes about behaviour and of belief, and while there is a clear pastoral concern, there is equally clear teaching about developing doctrine. Other letters follow much the same pattern.

The last book, 'The Revelation of John', is introduced in part by the words: 'Happy is the man who reads and happy those who listen to the words of this prophecy and heed what is written in it. For the hour of fulfilment is near.'

All this information in this form was inaccessible to the vast majority of the people for almost three-quarters of the Church's history to the present day. Its interpretation was in the hands of the priesthood and the educated few who could read and write. The main events of the life of Jesus were portrayed in pictures, stained glass and sculptures. The 'Stations of the Cross', in which the events surrounding the crucifixion are portrayed in a series of paintings or sculptures, is one of the best-known examples. The teaching content of the Gospels was more difficult to convey and, therefore, left scope for its interpretation to be developed without reference to the biblical text. For the last 550 years, translations and publications of the Bible have been available to an increasingly literate body who form the membership of the Churches. I believe, however, that a very great number of believers still rely for interpretation on trained clergy who, in turn, rely on theologians and biblical scholars. What follows, therefore, is not an innovation.

CHAPTER TWELVE The Teaching of Jesus as a Way of Life for Today

A contemporary summary of the teaching:

* All life is an expression of creative power. Each part has the potential for its own fulfilment. This creative power for human beings is described and experienced as love.
* All growth towards this end involves the exercise of power to realise it. Power can be used to control our environment, or free the elements that comprise it to reach their fulfilment.
* Human beings have an absolute capacity to make choices about their actions.
* The exercise of power to control or to allow others to make their own choices are legitimate in human society.
* We have freedom to make choices that may lead to either a threat or a benefit to our environment. This creates a need for the establishment of a system of law to control individual and community behaviour on the one hand, and, on the other, to encourage a love of life, of self-understanding, of care for others and for our environment.
* A legal system can lead to outcomes of security for a society and justice for individuals and communities within it, but inevitably creates conditions that militate against its purpose.
* A rule of law depends on systems of judgement and punishment to achieve its purpose. Imposing rules promotes aggressive attitudes and conflict.

Destructive social attitudes, including hypocrisy, evasion and deceit, are marks of the behaviour of those who do not obey the law.
* A society that depends on some to be rulers and others to obey creates the inevitability of the corruption of both leaders and subjects. This results in a continuous development of law, which, in turn, exacerbates its defects.
* We, with the power and freedom to make choices, have the capacity to participate consciously in our own growth and development.
* Individual human fulfilment is the outcome of self-understanding and commitment to the welfare of the whole environment.

Both self-understanding and freely offered commitment to others cannot be imposed and, therefore, do not rely on law. These attitudes are not self-generated but are an individual response to others. We learn to love by being loved. This depends on the existence of communities that live in this spirit to nurture us.

A loving society is based on the equal standing of its members. Some may have differing roles — as between parents and children and in wider community groups where individuals have different life skills and experience — but truly equal regard for others does not permit the formation of hierarchies.

Loving communities are not judgemental: they value understanding, compassion, honesty, trust and acceptance.

CHAPTER TWELVE The Teaching of Jesus as a Way of Life for Today

They promote individual and group security, confidence and adaptability.

Because of its nature, a loving community will never be large in number. The life it promotes and the values the participants hold depend on close fellowship and personal communication. They remain, however, a part of a total society and are able to exert a moderating influence on the damaging outcomes of the rule of law.

The formation of these communities calls from its participants an initial act of faith that a life of love will lead to personal and community fulfilment. The initial act of faith is reinforced by a whole-hearted commitment to this life.

This way of life is an ideal. To live a loving life, giving constant expression to an equal regard for others and ourselves, is, if not impossible, very difficult. The impediments are the assertion of what we think are our rights and a reliance on law to enforce them; our desire for material security; other competing interests of family and business; our lack of single-mindedness, of persistence and of self-discipline; our contrary emotions, such as envy, jealousy, anger and fear. The saving elements are the committed care of others for us, their acceptance of us, and their forgiveness of our damaging behaviour. In such a community, we experience the healing power of a loving community committed to an ideal and a life journey of faith, hope and love.

There is no judgement or punishment involved in this

journey, except that which we inflict on ourselves. The rewards of this life are experienced as we live it.

David sitting in his 'sermon-writing chair' in the study of the manse at Toorak Uniting Church.

PART THREE

CHAPTER THIRTEEN

The Experience of Wonder

David was inspired by the beauty of the natural world. He would have marvelled at this sunset appearing above our home in Glen Iris, Victoria, on Friday 7 May 2021.

I am aware and grateful that the scales of my life have been tilted towards the experience of being loved and of dreams being realised. I have been equally aware of and involved in a great deal of human disappointment and sorrow. I have learned that loving makes us very vulnerable. In times of hopelessness and depression there seems to be no prospect of future happiness.

Psalm 23 in the Old Testament concludes with the words of assurance that: '... goodness and mercy [love unfailing] shall follow me all the days of my life ...' The psalms are songs which, as today, are inspired by deeply felt experiences. These words, of course, were written long before Jesus was born. The author of this song, David, had clearly known times when he felt that goodness and love seemed to be far away. But he also knew that they were following him, that 'goodness and mercy' were still there for him. The psalm finishes: '... and I shall dwell in the house of the Lord forever.'

The 'house of the Lord' was the world he knew. Because he was a faithful shepherd, he was convinced that he also would be cared for — that was for him the nature of his life. Some Christian interpreters of David's song will accept this thought. Others, with knowledge of the life of Christ and the teaching of the Church, will maintain that the shepherd was in fact experiencing the work of the third member of the Trinity, the Holy Spirit. Still others will maintain this is supporting evidence for the pre-existing Christ and for John's Gospel, which declares: 'When all things began the Word already was ... So the Word became flesh; he came to dwell among us and we saw his glory.'

So much for the development of doctrine and dogma, when all we need to know is that, as Christians, we believe that each of us, in our humanity, is able through love to

CHAPTER THIRTEEN The Experience of Wonder

counteract evil and dispel the fear in the world in which we live.

How can we be sure of this? The simple answer is to have faith. It is easier for those who have been deeply nurtured by love. It becomes more difficult when we experience the dark side of faith, our doubt. What I have called 'the experience of wonder' leads us beyond our fears. It is like standing on a mountaintop and being able to see the whole world and sense its oneness, not in some fantasy future, but here and now.

I have said that my parents were conventional Christians. By that I mean that in matters of belief they did not question their faith. I very rarely talked to them about it. My mother, who was essentially practical and deeply committed to her life of compassionate service, only once rebuffed me. Someone close to her had unexpectedly died. As she told me about it, she said, 'Well, it's not for us to question it. We all come to it in God's time and it must be for the best.' My adolescent reply — to the effect that it was not for the best, and that God really had nothing to do with it — met with an unusually abrupt and dismissive response, and the discussion was closed. My comment had clearly upset her deeply. Only years later, as I recall it, I think I understand what lay behind her reaction. The foundation of her faith was a belief that whatever happened somehow fitted the pattern of God's purpose. Life was like a great jigsaw puzzle and in the end every isolated or strange-looking part of it — even if only a fragment — would be part of the whole.

That is what the idea of heaven is about. I believe that the idea is legitimate, but that heaven is located in the wrong place. An experience of wholeness, which is the literal meaning of salvation and includes the idea of heaven, is part of the life we can know here and now. The promise of heaven as an eventual reward is the thief of that reality. It is a barrier to present contentment and the opportunity for fulfilment and peace.

I remember well a woman whom I met in her later years and who became a great and close friend. She was unmarried, vital and attractive, generous and interesting. I was her minister. Though we had many conversations, religion was never discussed. Her faith was taken for granted by both of us. A time came when a long-term health problem became an incurable illness. She assured me that she was not afraid of dying, but that she was disappointed. Unlike her earlier life, her later years had been so fulfilled and so happy that it was a terrible thing to have to let go. She went on to say, 'But at least I can look forward to seeing my father and mother, and my brother and many friends again.' What could I say? It was a time only for loving acceptance. But I still grieve for her that she did not have a sense of wholeness present all the days of her life.

I believe that there are moments in our present life when we can experience a sense of completeness, of being a part of the whole. That awareness is not for me like a continuous realisation. It is more like a very occasional

CHAPTER THIRTEEN The Experience of Wonder

lifting of a veil, a vision if you like, that once seen is never forgotten. In my varied reading, I have recognised this experience and learned to describe it as being 'surprised by joy'. In that moment one feels a sense of wonder that one truly is a fragment of a whole and complete universe. Being surprised by joy takes many forms, but that is the common thread.

I have suggested that the faculty of awareness is observable in species other than human beings, but that it has become, through our development of language and culture, a much more heightened faculty, experienced and described by many as the life of the spirit. I believe that what the teaching of Jesus calls eternal life is the journey towards ever-increasing awareness. The following accounts may not be accepted as evidence that can be tested, but they are nevertheless revealing and supportive of this claim.

Some time after the poet Wordsworth's young daughter died, he wrote:

Surprised by joy — impatient as the Wind
I turned to share the transport — Oh! with whom
But Thee, long buried in the silent Tomb.

C. S. Lewis, one of the greatest apologists for Christianity in the middle of the 20th century, took Wordsworth's phrase, 'Surprised by joy', as the title of his autobiography. When he was a young boy, his older brother one day brought into their nursery a toy garden, which he had built into the lid of an old biscuit tin. Here were just the fragments of a garden — moss, pebbles and twigs. But he remembered that, as he looked at it, it seemed to contain the whole of creation. It seemed to expand and enfold him in an ecstasy of being beyond the reach of words. He knew himself to be at one with the beginning and end of all things. For the first time in his life, he had been 'surprised by joy'.

In 1946, soon after the end of the Second World War and, when in the middle of an arts degree, I was standing in an upstairs room looking out at two trees being tossed by the wind, when I suddenly felt as though the walls of the room had been dissolved and I was caught up in a feeling of completeness, of being part of the whole universe. It wasn't a prolonged moment, but as my familiar environment slipped back into place, I was left with a great sense of inward peace. I later realised that I had been surprised by joy.

Morris West, whose final book, *The Last Confession*, was almost completed when he died at his desk in October 1999, tells the story of Giordano Bruno, a Dominican monk who, after a seven-year interrogation by the Inquisition in the last days of the 16th century, was burned at the stake as a heretic in Rome in 1600 AD. It is a novel based on fact but written in the form of a diary kept by Bruno in those last years. In Bruno's words:

> Seven years of prison and prison diet have sapped my strength and dimmed my desire ...

CHAPTER THIRTEEN The Experience of Wonder

Yet I still remember that night ... for the strange and quite magical moment of revelation which I experienced in the small hours of the morning ... I stood naked at the window, looking out at a clear winter sky, full of bright stars. Suddenly I understood what I needed to say, what I had been trying to say all those years in Latin, in Italian, in writing and by word of mouth, but which I had not been able to articulate fully.

I was no longer — human kind was no longer — locked in the close circle of Ptolemy's or Copernicus's universe. We were not at the centre of it either. We were not a single system, we were the smallest part of a vast creation, expanding to infinity ... This, it seemed to me, was the final coda of the revelation. We were not separate. Nothing in the cosmos was separate or disconnected ... None of it could fall out of the hands of the Creator who had made it, had infused it, and was immanent in all its parts.

Montserrat Caballé, the renowned opera singer, said:
I was born with a voice. But this isn't enough to make me a singer ... A singer's vocal cords are not that different from a normal person's. It must therefore come from somewhere else, or rather, everywhere else, inside. I also believe that music, sound waves, are everywhere around us. Why

don't we hear them? Because we are not yet ready to. We are still too deeply immersed in matter and have as yet developed only a tiny part of our mind potential ... When we evolve even further, we will become aware of the state of union that binds us to everything in creation and be able to hear, to be inside and part of the music around us without having to 'make' it ... The body is a concrete thing ... but when you are in this state of fusion with music you are totally unaware of it. You feel light, weightless, and afterwards, boom, you feel so heavy again ... I don't know why this happens or how to explain it, but I know that it does and that audiences feel it, too.

Caballé has also been surprised by joy.

Just before Christmas Day 2004, a friend of mine described how she and her granddaughter made a model of the nativity scene:

We had our baby, wrapped in swaddling clothes and we laid him in a manger. My old head and the young one touched as we gazed in silent concentration at our creation. Like millions of others down the centuries we had made our own image, albeit from a button and scraps of paper, a story of love and hope. A story my grandchild had a right to know. I put my arm around Mairead and we smiled at each other, surprised

CHAPTER THIRTEEN   The Experience of Wonder

by joy in a timeless fragment of our lives, a time remembered. It was Christmas Eve.

Fifty-six years ago, I was a student and over 12,000 miles from home. Subjected to a rigorous analysis of the belief I had always accepted simply, I began to feel my faith slip from me, and with my faith, my trust, and with my trust, my confidence. One day we were singing the 23rd Psalm as grace after lunch in college when I looked up and saw the face of the man opposite me. His name was Akuffo. He came as a postgraduate student from what was then known as the African Gold Coast. I can describe his face as I saw it in that moment only as black radiance as, with such trust, he sang that song of David. The light that flowed out from him flowed into me. Although I have never thought of myself as a mystic and I don't think that I am, I know now that I was again surprised by joy. In that moment, the whole of my faith and my being made sense, though I couldn't have described the feeling then.

If we are not sometimes caught up in a moment of wonder, surprised by joy, it may be that we have traded our freedom for our security; that seeing a vision of what we can be, of what faith in our own humanity can give us, of what the Church could be, we have also seen the risks. There are risks in following visions. Then we have run back to our own Egypt, crying with our faithless forebears, 'Better to be a slave in Egypt, than die in the wilderness.'

Joy is the companion of each of us who has been set free from fear and known love made real.

I am sure that, when Jesus said a childlike acceptance of life was the way into its fullness, he was implying that when we are loved as children we are open to wonder. As we grow older, our experience of disappointment and fear blunts and erodes that gift.

In many ways, the misunderstanding of Jesus' teaching, the legal, institutional forms that have presented it and the moral attitudes which that misinterpretation has encouraged, have damaged this gift. The stories I have recounted are repeated in many ways, in poetry, in novels, in experiences of which others tell me. They are indicators of the promise of a fulfilled life, which break through our daily routines and illuminate them. Wonder is a gateway to faith that the whole creation moves towards completion, and that we, tiny fractions of life, are nevertheless made whole in being part of it.

This is not a matter of empty speculation, but the claim has to be given substance. While wonder is a gateway to faith, reformation of the Christian Churches, which claim to declare the truth about life, is a very practical and demanding business. Embarking on it, we need to remain open to wonder.

CHAPTER THIRTEEN   The Experience of Wonder

David loved Australian native plants. Two of these magnificent *Eucalyptus citriodora* were planted by him in 1987 in the park adjacent to our former home.

The beautiful *Eucalyptus ficifolia* and two forms of the *Callistemon citrinus*, 'White Anzac' and 'Endeavour' are in our current garden in Glen Iris.

PART FOUR

CHAPTER FOURTEEN

Reclaiming the Church as a Human Heritage

To reclaim the Church as a human heritage is an impossibility for those who believe that it has been built on the foundation of an interventionist, supernatural being who has created and rules the universe. To reclaim the Church as a human heritage, which is built on the life and teaching of the man Jesus, is the business of reformation. Those who reject the divine and accept the human heritage have a legitimate claim to a belief that the Church has been stolen from them.

I believe that a very large number of those with a Christian and Church background, who are now estranged from the communities that have nurtured them in the past, will welcome the position I, and others, have taken.

I am aware that a great many leaders and members of the Church will dismiss it as outrageous and reject it without any further thought. However, I re-assert my claim that it is not a rejection of Jesus and his teaching. It is a rejection of the way in which the young Church adopted from its Jewish heritage the doctrines of monotheism and divine law.

The only parable of Jesus recorded in the fourth Gospel is that of the good shepherd. John places it in his account as an introduction to the events of the last days of Jesus' life. The words in brackets indicate the theistic setting of the Gospel. The translation is *The New English Bible.* John 10: 1–21:

> In truth I tell you, in very truth, the man who does not enter the sheepfold by the door, but climbs in some other way, is nothing but a thief or a robber. The man who enters by the door is the shepherd in charge of the sheep. The door-keeper admits him, and the sheep hear his voice; he calls his own sheep by name, and leads them out. When he has brought them all out, he goes ahead and the sheep follow, because they know his voice. They will not follow a stranger; they will run away from him, because they do not recognise the voice of strangers.

This was a parable that Jesus told them, but they did not understand what he meant by it. So Jesus spoke again:

> In truth, in very truth I tell you, I am the door of the sheepfold. The sheep paid no heed to any who came before me, for these were all thieves and robbers. I am the door; anyone who comes into the fold through me shall be safe. He shall go in and out and shall find pasturage.

CHAPTER FOURTEEN Reclaiming the Church as a Human Heritage

The thief comes only to steal, to kill, to destroy; I have come that men may have life, and may have it in all its fullness. I am the good shepherd; the good shepherd lays down his life for his sheep. The hireling, when he sees the wolf coming, abandons the sheep and runs away, because he is no shepherd and the sheep are not his. Then the wolf harries the flock and scatters the sheep. The man runs away because he is a hireling and cares nothing for the sheep.

I am the good shepherd; I know my own sheep and my sheep know me — (as the Father knows me and I know the Father) — and I lay down my life for the sheep. But there are other sheep of mine, not belonging to this fold, whom I must bring in; and they too will listen to my voice. There will then be one flock, one shepherd. (The Father loves me because) I lay down my life, to receive it back again. No-one has robbed me of it; I am laying it down of my own free will. I have the right to lay it down, and I have the right to receive it back again; (this charge I have received from my Father).

When reading this parable, omitting the bracketed words, the theistic insertions are revealed. They appear to be fairly clumsy interruptions to this clarifying story that Jesus offers at the request of his hearers. It also reveals the fully human content of his teaching and links very closely with the last words of Jesus to his disciples.

How then should we think of and describe Jesus? I remember one of my teachers saying that there were only three possible answers to that question. He was either mad, bad or divine. For me the options do not stop there. He was neither mad, bad nor divine. He was human. Not even 'unique human' for that sets him, in essence, apart from us. One could use many words: wise, loving, courageous, prophetic. I think of him as the ideal human in whom love was made real for all people and all time. His teaching and example compel my allegiance and my commitment to the truth he taught and lived.

CHAPTER FIFTEEN

A Place to Start

Some who have left their Church may advocate offering support to the creation of a new one. That is not a possible outcome of the position I have taken. I am not advocating revolution. This is for one central reason: I believe that the Christian Churches, despite their history, have maintained the essential record of the life and teaching of Jesus. Distorted it, betrayed it, misused it, but not destroyed it.

Through the years, men and women have sought to reform the Churches' teachings and some have literally given their lives to that end.

One of the great principles from the 16th century is that the Church is always being reformed. Many movements have led to what has seemed an unavoidable separation. This applies particularly to major divisions in the pre-Reformation Church in which Martin Luther and John Calvin are pre-eminent. In the growth of the ecumenical movement in the 20th century, significant initiatives have led to discussions across this major divide.

More voices are being heard saying that for all Christian Churches there must be unity or death.

The main reason for my commitment as a Presbyterian minister to the cause of the union of Methodists, Congregationalists and Presbyterians was that their separation in Australia, whatever their differences in government, and to a much smaller extent in doctrine, was of little importance compared with the fact that those who declared their faith in a reconciling Gospel had to be reconciled to one another.

It was motivated by the same conviction that I now hold even more strongly: the desire to see love made real.

I also appreciate how fortunate I have been in the congregations to which I have ministered. My ordination vows required me to confess my belief in God. I expressed that in worship and beyond it in good faith in meeting expectations of me. I am aware that some people who read this will possibly label my ministry as hypocritical. To that accusation, I will respond in three ways.

Firstly, in my preaching, I encouraged those who heard me to question their faith. I remember a sermon that I titled 'Doubt, the Other Side of Faith'. In the following week, I received a letter from an extremely successful and very generous man who said that he was deeply comforted by what he had heard, and that he was reassured by the fact that his minister understood and shared his thoughts and his feelings. Secondly, in human terms, I believe that the congregations which I served, in their support of the

CHAPTER FIFTEEN A Place to Start

community programs that we created, acted in faithful response to the Gospel: to the teaching and example of the man Jesus. Thirdly, I lived within the idiom of my own generation. This is what I have suggested was the reason that Jesus, whom I believe did not accept the theistic foundation of his generation, still expressed himself in its religious idiom.

It will be maintained that I, with others, by taking a position of rejecting theism and the whole supernatural doctrinal teaching that flows from it, are advocating not reform but abolition of the Church. My response is that this is a fundamental reformation of Christianity as the Churches have taught it. It is not a suggested reformation of some aspects of a particular Church, but of all of the Christian Churches.

All reformations have a historical setting and reflect that in their advocacy. One obvious example is the English Reformation in its separation from Rome to fulfil the personal desires and ambitions of Henry VIII.

The reformation I advocate has a specific historical setting, of which one of the major elements is the scientific nature of our age. The distortion of the teaching of Jesus in the first century Church reflects the knowledge of the time: belief in the supernatural and, for Israel, in one God and the rule of Divine Law. The only difference in this proposal for reformation from all the others is that it is not partial, but total.

The Uniting Church in Australia, created in 1977, and

building on 16th and 17th century reformation principles, includes in the Basis of Union the following statements:

> That the three Churches entering into Union ... praise God for his gifts of grace to each of them in years past; they acknowledge that none of them has responded to God's love with a full obedience; they look for a continuing renewal ... To this end they declare their readiness to go forward together in sole loyalty to Christ ... they remain open to constant reform under his Word ... These Churches commit their members to acknowledge one another in love and joy as believers in Our Lord Jesus Christ ... [Paragraph 1]
>
> Recalling the Ecumenical Councils of the early centuries, she looks forward to a time when faith will be further elucidated ... [Paragraph 2]

In the great majority of reformation movements in the Christian Church, the initiative has come from those whose lives have been most closely linked to its organisation and are most familiar with its teaching. The emphasis has been laid on issues of doctrine and government. My experience has been that a majority of members of the Church, who have not been involved in these areas, accept, without much scrutiny, the guidance of their leaders.

The Iona Community of Scotland was founded in 1938 by George MacLeod after his experience in an industrial parish in Glasgow. Its aim was to bring the Church into closer touch with the industrial and working life of Scotland. It operated

CHAPTER FIFTEEN A Place to Start

in its early life outside the structures of the Church. It was in many ways radical in its approach and widely criticised by elements within the established Church of Scotland. George MacLeod was fond of saying, 'In the Church of Scotland, the Elders used to take their brains off with their hats as they entered the church door.'

I am not making that assertion about the lay men and women of today. I once spoke to a senior scientist of one of our universities, whom I know agrees that the theistic doctrine, the concept of a supernatural God, is no longer tenable. I asked him how he reconciled this with his continuing attendance at his local church services. He replied with a smile that he simply transposed the content into non-theistic terms. I don't think that he is alone.

Again, my experience has shown me that the major motivations to become and remain a member of a congregation are family background and tradition, the security of a community of shared values, a desire for their children to be influenced by that experience, and the opportunity to live a life in which interest and care for others is possible.

These influences are not as strong as they were more than fifty years ago in the middle of the 20th century. For many, family traditions have been weakened; value systems have been challenged by wider education; and a more materialistic society, as well as our growing urban environment, have tended to adversely affect the growth of local communities.

None of this alters the fact that the Churches are still committed to the life and teaching of Jesus as the truth, and that this is most clearly expressed in the many who try to live by it, in families, in personal relationships, in congregations of the Church, and in individual involvement in the secular world.

The reformation for our time will not be primarily promoted by those who are established by law in the institutional life of the Churches. It will, in a major way, be in the hands of those men and women who are wherever they may be, as members of congregations or outside them, trying to make love real for themselves and others.

The rejection of the concept of theism, and of the rule of law in the ordering of the life of the Church, would have a major effect on the form of its life beyond congregations. The Uniting Church, in adopting a conciliar form of government in 1977, sought to avoid the creation of hierarchies, but in the almost thirty years of its existence, has not been freed from a tendency towards the control exercised by a central bureaucracy and increasing legislation.

The nature of gathered life within a congregation would be enhanced. I believe that it would have greater integrity. Its inspiration would be commitment to the teaching of Jesus, the expectation of a fulfilling experience in the present, the hope of a greater happiness for individuals and communities in the future, and the celebration of a loving life. It is unrealistic, however, to think that the Churches, as they are, would welcome this reform. It would be argued that to do

CHAPTER FIFTEEN A Place to Start

so would be to destroy Christianity as a religion and replace it with a philosophy: to reject God and replace the concept with a human ideal. That argument is, for me, too simple. True reform would destroy Christianity as a religion, but it would not destroy faith in the teaching of Jesus.

As I write, parts of Australia are in the grip of drought. We hear that a leader of one major Christian Church is calling his people to pray to God for rain. At the same time, I hear a meteorologist broadcasting the possibility of some rain in the near future, and making a cynical reference to the part prayer may play in it. This prayer may be justified if one believes in a God who intervenes for the benefit of His creation, but for most people today, Christian or not, it is absolute nonsense. This may be an extreme example of theistic faith, but it is one of many similar examples that cause people to dismiss the teaching of the Churches. My great concern is that, in rightly rejecting the nonsense, great numbers of people also reject the teaching of Jesus and the communities of faith that have nurtured it.

In 1949, my first year as a theological student, *The Misunderstanding of the Church* was published by Emil Brunner, a Swiss theologian. In it, he likened the Church to a nut, describing it as having a very hard outer covering that was designed to protect and nurture the sweet kernel. He argued that it sometimes happened that the husk in the nut thickened and crushed the kernel. In the Church, he maintained, the outer covering of law was in danger of destroying the kernel of the Gospel. I am not advocating the destruction of the husk, but of creating a sensitive membrane to protect and nurture its heart.

There are many possibilities for the creation of communities that will cultivate a loving life, both within and without them. They may exist in and around the Churches many of us know and to which we have committed our lives. More importantly, those who believe in their potential to make love real, but have had no experience of the life and teaching of Jesus, may discover a means of fulfilling their hopes and desires.

CHAPTER SIXTEEN

Not a New Church but a Reformed One

In these final chapters, I want to consider the possible form of a Church that would reflect the views that I have expressed.

The design of a legal system is based on the need to create order in a community where there are competing interests. This applies to any rule of law, secular or religious.

This is less obvious than it was many years ago. In the records from a previous era of the administration of St Giles' Cathedral in Edinburgh is the account of a member of the parish who had been convicted of an offence. The punishment, decreed by the elders, was that he would wear a penitent's sheet and be seated at the entrance of the cathedral for a specified number of weeks, as the members of the congregation passed by. It was an ecclesiastical form of the stocks. His weekly presence was noted until, part way into his sentence, it was recorded that he went mad and was removed to an asylum. As it was perceived then, one of the functions of the church was to maintain moral standards and this was reflected in its administration.

In our time, Christian homosexual men and women are, in some instances, refused communion and, in some Churches, denied any participation in the priesthood or ministry. The action of turning individuals away from a service of the Church and refusing requests for training for ministry is the form that reflects the perceived moral content of Christian teaching today. It is certainly not a form that makes love real.

All societies benefit from order. The ordering of the life of a loving community operates on different levels. On the level of emotional life, it springs from the desire to relate to others affectionately as friends, within a family or sexually. Our feelings are the driving force in forming and ordering these relationships. Our feelings also largely determine their maintenance and duration. The driving force behind the formation of communities broader than these emotionally inspired ones is a search for purpose in life beyond more intimate limits and a desire to pursue it. These motivations are not exclusive. Both emotional and rational factors are involved in all our actions. In general terms, however, the wider the limits of the community, the greater the necessity of an act of will to be involved in it.

Ordered life in a family may arise quite simply out of common expectations. Parents and their children both contribute to a loving family by meeting each others' expectations, which are expressed and agreed. This

CHAPTER SIXTEEN   Not a New Church but a Reformed One

applies in different degrees to affection, friendship, family and sexual love. There is harmony when these loves are equally reciprocated. In reality, however, even when a relationship in these terms is strong, divisive factors that threaten harmony may arise. Living a loving life as the accepted foundation of any community will do more than create its own order. The freely offered commitment to its life will generate a spirit and power within the group, which will endow its individual members with the ability to transcend the negative human responses that are also part of our animal nature.

Love of life, love of self, love of others and care for our environment form the foundation of loving communities. Within any community there will be bonds of affection, of friendship and of sexual love, but there will also be many who do not experience these personal ties in a group. The desire to build a relationship with others is also primarily created by common beliefs and values. In this latter case, a community will be created with a more deliberate purpose and its order more specifically defined.

An important principle of design is that form should follow function. In architecture, a design for a building should not only take its environment into account but should reflect the activity it will contain. In designing a garden, the environment suited to the growth of particular plants is a fundamental aspect. The same principle applies to the design of a community. The design of a system of law is based on the need to create order in a society in which some individuals or groups wish to benefit themselves at the expense of others. This involves provision for the making of laws, their administration and the judgement of those who break them, and the punishment of offenders.

In the mainstream of Churches in the Western world, the same principle has been applied. There is provision at various levels for the making of law, its administration and the judgement and punishment of those who offend against it. The basis of this call for a reformation of the Church is that the teaching of Jesus is incompatible with the legal form that the Churches have adopted. The rule of law and a life ordered by love are incompatible. In a reformed faith community, its function must be reflected by its form.

In considering in more specific detail the form of the life of a Church that is inspired by the teaching of Jesus, it is necessary to establish the principles on which it will be founded:

* There will be an acceptance of the rule of law in the wider society of which the Church is a part. There will be a conviction that this necessary rule of law, which relies on the control of individuals and groups through the imposition of penalties, cannot by its nature provide an environment in which order is created in a community through the free commitment of its members.
* There will also be a conviction that, while there is a clear separation between two such societies, each may

benefit from the other. The rule of law may result in the provision of the freedom for groups living within but beyond it. The life of a free community may restrain the creation and imposition of unjust laws.

* Communities following the teaching of Jesus will celebrate the spirit of life that is expressed through all forms of creation.
* This spirit will be expressed through the lives of individuals who, separately and together, will commit themselves to an understanding of their own potential, a life of love for others, and loving care of their whole environment.
* Individuals within a community life will be equally valued.
* Every form of life will be valued for itself.
* Individuals who express a desire to join a community will be under no obligations or rules.
* Communities will determine their own form of life.

CHAPTER SEVENTEEN

Belief and Ritual

Rituals play a large part in our daily life. They are rich in symbolism, which varies from the simple and private to the complex and public. The simple and private may be as individual as, for example, the choice of clothes to wear. Public rituals vary from the informal, such as the chants at games between the supporters of opposing teams, to planned marriage celebrations and highly structured state funerals. The public may be as elaborate as the ritual surrounding the death of a pope, which, as I am writing, has been exposed to the world [April, 2005].

Symbols, both private and public, are designed to express the essence of the occasion, or the truth symbolised. One of the visible signs of change in our life is the modification or change in the symbols. The celebration of the Christian beliefs in the birth and death of Jesus is an example. One of the more contentious issues in Australian society at the moment is whether the nativity rituals surrounding the birth of Jesus in our pre-school education for children is a true expression of our multicultural, multi-religious society.

CHAPTER SEVENTEEN Belief and Ritual

I remember seeing a pre-Easter billboard, a number of years ago, which was advertising a clothing firm. It depicted an outstretched open hand holding a chicken, with the caption '... presents Easter'. For Christians, Easter is a celebration of death and resurrection, so that there is a slight connection between a chicken and a celebration of new life, but tenuous only, and not as a symbol of a fundamental belief. This is not a modern development. The Christian Church in its early years celebrated the birth of Jesus on the day celebrated in its contemporary world as the birthday of the sun god Mithras, which was associated with the winter solstice. For sun worshippers, it symbolised the end of long, dark days. Christians would have seen a connection to their belief in the birth of Jesus.

Because symbols are so powerful, great care must be taken in creating them. In the final year of our training at New College, Edinburgh, we were required to preach what was called a 'trial sermon'. One of my friends, who went on to become a well-known preacher in Scotland, was allocated a date in April. He, very compellingly, developed a theme on the conjunction of Easter and spring — of the resurrection of Jesus and the emergence of new life in nature. I congratulated him, but couldn't resist reminding him that in the southern hemisphere we celebrated Easter as winter approached.

If beliefs change, symbols must change. Most of the rituals of the Church are deeply and firmly embedded in theism. The architecture is designed to accommodate it. Roman Catholic doctrine teaches that in the mass the priests are the mediators between the people and God. God's presence is symbolised by the altar and in the celebration of the mass. In Reformed doctrine, God's presence is celebrated in the gathered people, the open Bible and the communion service. In Reformed architecture, the altar is replaced by a table around which the people gather and, in some traditions, the pulpit, from which the minister expounds the Bible, is placed behind the table and significantly elevated above it. Numerous writers have said that, in many ways, the Reformation was born on the wings of literacy as the result of the invention of the printing press and of translations of the Bible into indigenous languages. When people were able to compare the Church's practice with the text of the Bible, they were in a position to question it. In Reformed Churches, the centrality of the mass was challenged and rituals modified to give greater prominence to the teaching: the sermon, which was based on the biblical text.

In the Reformed tradition, and particularly the Calvinist, although some symbols were maintained, many were abolished or changed. The re-enactment of the Last Supper of Jesus with his disciples included the same elements as the Catholic mass, and the symbols in the sacrament of baptism have been retained. On the other hand, the veneration of Mary, the mother of Jesus, and of the saints was abolished and the statues and pictures associated with them removed.

CHAPTER SEVENTEEN Belief and Ritual

While these changes were not simply cosmetic ones, they did not change the essential truth that was symbolically celebrated in worship. That truth was, and is, for the mainstream Christian Western Churches, that a supernatural being who created the universe had revealed himself in a man, Jesus, whose teaching and life ensured salvation and a future life with God in heaven for those who believed and accepted him as God's son.

If we can no longer retain a theistic belief, but are committed to the teaching and example of the man Jesus, and wish and need to celebrate that conviction, we must find new ways to do it.

For many years, those who are concerned with liturgy, the content of a service of worship — theologians and scholars, priests and ministers — have struggled with the fact that younger people who have retained some connection with the Church through its activities have demonstrated an indifference to its forms of worship. New symbols, youth services, contemporary music, dialogues in place of sermons, informal settings and the rest have come and gone with varied appeal; but the Church, like 'Ol' Man River', just keeps rolling along. The mighty river of Church adherence in the dawn of the 2000s is dwindling fast. The parents of the absentee children cling to their belief in Christian life and morality, but have become almost as indifferent as their offspring to its ritual practice.

Why? Because while they and their children would still claim to be Christian and continue to practise what they believe is a Christian life, they simply do not believe in the existence of a supernatural God, or participate with any true integrity in occasions that celebrate it.

A new reformation will produce a new liturgy and the river of belief and commitment will broaden and deepen again.

CHAPTER EIGHTEEN

Living a Loving Life

[This chapter and the one following share similar thoughts. Both are included here for comparison.]

Because form should follow and reflect content, I want to outline my concept of a community where love is made real. These communities, of course, exist now: in families, in friendships, in many and varied groups. All of these have a specific base. I envisage a universal base where all who seek it are accepted and welcomed.

Living a loving life is not easy — one which not only embraces our own families, friends, colleagues and those who share our interests, but reaches out to embrace all. We have our own unloving attitudes, both towards ourselves and others. In limited-sized, loving associations like families, we are often helped to overcome these, but if we want to love universally, we need to be more widely loved and supported.

It will be a community based on human knowledge and experience. Central to these is the life and teaching of Jesus recorded in the first four books of the New Testament contained in the Bible. It will be recognised that these accounts are open to interpretation, but that there are basic elements on which the teaching rests. These include the injunction to love others as Jesus, in his life, has loved; to respect the necessity for the exercise of law in the conduct of society; to create and maintain a community that is not ordered by law, but by the ongoing commitment to the example of his love.

A typical community, as I envisage it, will follow two broad directions, which I would describe as a journey inwards and a journey outwards. The journey inwards will encourage and support individuals whose desire and commitment are to lead a loving life. The journey outwards will encourage and support individuals and groups to become increasingly aware of and active in their total environment.

Group cohesion will be deepened and energised by the exercise of rituals. They could include appreciation of life in all its forms; the happiness in loving and being loved; the joyous response to music and all the arts; the growth of knowledge and understanding of ourselves and others.

Aspects of the journey inwards may include the encouragement of self-knowledge and personal growth in which meditation may be practised; the recommended access, when sought, to counselling and medical help; the provision of information and books dealing with these issues.

CHAPTER EIGHTEEN   Living a Loving Life

Aspects of the journey outwards may include the development of personal human relationship skills; encouragement of knowledge about, and care for, the physical environment; an interest in chosen areas of scientific research, of religions and philosophies, of conservation societies, of government policies, of the planning of housing and community facilities and infrastructure.

This may seem to constitute a very large agenda for a small group. It is not suggested that equal commitment would be made to each part. The particular interests of members will constitute the detail of any program. This outline will be developed and varied freely according to the life of the group.

The content will suggest and indicate the form of the community. Participation will be organised in such a way that individuals will be able to create and maintain close relationships with all others in a group. The psychology of group formation indicates that four units of seven to nine, making a total of twenty-eight to thirty-six, is the optimum way to achieve this cohesion. This may be duplicated to accommodate larger numbers in a single community.

There will be no criteria for membership other than an individual desire to join the community. Leadership in such a community will be shared by all the participants and will vary according to the activity. Individuals will have different skills, which will become apparent and recognised. Decisions affecting the life of any group will be made by all participants meeting together and seeking consensus.

The administration of a community will be a voluntary function. If a community grows sufficiently beyond one small group to warrant the creation of further groups, the same voluntary administration may facilitate any relationship between them. If a number of groups are formed from different sources, which would require coordination, it may be necessary to appoint a paid administrator.

Local communities, while they maintain their independence, may be confronted by some difficulties and be unable to take advantage of some opportunities.

One of the major difficulties is likely to be centred on the fact that some participants will identify so closely with their place in the group that they will feel easily challenged by others who do not share their perception of that position. This is likely to precipitate competition between individuals. In a community that has access to rules and regulations, these may provide some sort of procedure and solution. It is not, however, likely to solve the personal issues involved. The alternative is in some ways more difficult. It calls for a willingness among the participants to accept the situation, to discuss it freely, and to work towards a resolution until it is reached. How this is achieved is the task of the whole group in every case. The journey towards this has the potential for individual and community enrichment and growth.

CHAPTER EIGHTEEN   Living a Loving Life

Another difficulty that may be encountered is that interest in one aspect of a group's life may be followed to the exclusion of others. In a legal structure, this may be addressed by reference to a constitution and the refining of regulations, but it will not resolve the difficulty and is more likely to result in separation than in unity. Once again, the caring journey that a group takes towards resolution has the possibility for enrichment and growth.

The opportunities for small independent groups to learn from others and to take any desired action for which they do not have the resources may be lost, without the opportunity to build links between communities. Commonly, the Churches and similar organisations deal with this by creating centralised structures, which are designed and regulated to service this need. The danger, often realised, is that the small, scattered groups receive inadequate assistance and the central structure makes growing demands for its own maintenance. More dangerously, the hierarchy created develops its own ethos and seeks to impose it on the scattered groups. The principle of voluntary cooperation is valid. Its implementation will not be negotiable by law or regulation. This is vitally important and difficult, but not impossible to achieve.

I have maintained that I am not advocating the creation of a new Church. The first difficult obstacle is to establish a way in which this call for reformation may be heard and discussed in the ongoing life of the Churches we know. In many congregations there are existing study and discussion groups. I am aware that, in some instances, the subjects chosen are based on books that present the same anti-theistic view that I have developed here. My hope is that in the Uniting Church, at least, such discussion may be encouraged.

I have not written this book for academic philosophers, theologians or church historians, but for an interested, educated and, maybe, disappointed or alienated laity. If discussion leads to a desire to establish a group associated with an existing congregation, this would call for a mutual arrangement to prevent any sense of divisiveness between the two groups.

If these proposals seem to be an impossible dream, the alternative may well be a possible nightmare for all who are committed to the teaching of Jesus and to a life lived to make their love real. Those who live in the Churches as they are, and those who look for reform, may well, in their separate ways, be a living denial of the Gospel of the reconciling love they proclaim.

CHAPTER NINETEEN

A Spirit of Life Community

The Formation of Groups

Different communities will always give varying emphasis to aspects of their life. There will, however, be a shared basis in the teaching of Jesus. Accepting the principle that form should follow content, the communities will exhibit some distinctive marks:

* A community will be small enough to allow significant knowledge of individuals to be shared by all others in the group. The psychology of group life indicates that the most effective, and therefore the easiest to maintain towards this end, is a number of approximately thirty. Beyond a number of fifty, a different and less personal dynamic operates.
* Full communication within a group depends on each member having a maximum opportunity to contribute. This is best achieved within a group of seven to nine.
* Effective action depends on available resources. These are more readily available through the cooperation of larger groups.

* Leadership in any group will be a shared role by all participants. It will not be formalised, but established by the recognition and acceptance of individual talents appropriate to the purpose of the group.
* In any community or federation of communities for particular purposes, the services of an administrator may be necessary. This function will be determined by and responsible to the community or communities that have sponsored it.

ACTIVITY WITHIN A COMMUNITY

Within each community, expression will be given to its life in four ways: appreciation of the gift of life; encouragement of self-knowledge and personal growth; concern for and care of others; and encouragement of knowledge of the environment and care for it.

* The celebration of life may include rituals, which include appreciation of life in all its forms: the wonder of the life-force in the whole creation; the happiness experienced in loving and being loved; the joyous response to music and all the arts; the growth of knowledge and understanding of ourselves and others.
* The encouragement of self-knowledge and personal growth will include ways in which reflection and meditation may be practised; the recommended access, when sought, to counselling and medical

CHAPTER NINETEEN A Spirit of Life Community

help; the provision of information and books dealing with these issues.

* The development of concern for and care of others will be the outcome of the maintenance of a group life that is accepting, understanding and non-judgemental. It may take many forms, including the care of others in the Spirit of Life Community, the encouragement of interest in neighbours and colleagues, and the support of those affected temporarily or permanently by crises.

The encouragement of knowledge about, and care for, the environment will include an interest in chosen areas of scientific research: of religions and philosophies, of conservation societies, of government policies, and of the planning of housing and community facilities and infrastructure.

This list may seem to constitute a very large agenda for a small group. It is not suggested that equal commitment should be made to each part. The particular interests of members will constitute the detail of any program. It is proposed, however, that these four areas of commitment be recognised in the life of a community.

CHAPTER TWENTY

In Conclusion

Since I retired from full-time ministry, I have remained in close touch with many friends, a number of whom have known me as their minister. Some have stayed within the community of the Church, but most have moved on. In the last few years, I have organised some informal discussion groups, which have included a wider group whose experience of religion has led them in different directions. They include those who have adopted a different faith, some from different Christian denominations and some with no connection to religion. Individually, they have professional backgrounds in science, sociology, human sciences, medicine, business, teaching, writing and music. Together we share a commitment to making sense of the world in which we live.

What I have written is my contribution to that search. As I have indicated, it is in part the story of my life. I was once asked how I would describe my experience as a minister. My answer was that I had for many years lived day by day through a continuous series of interruptions about personal

CHAPTER TWENTY In Conclusion

concerns, administrative demands, planning programs, and pastoral concerns including counselling, weddings and funerals. I am aware now that while my experience could be seen as a series of disruptions, it nevertheless had its own unity. My constant endeavour was in every situation to try to make love real for myself and others. On many occasions I failed.

Recently, there was a message on my answering machine, which took me back more than twenty-five years. It was from a mother whose daughter, I think, was planning to marry for a second time and who had said to her, 'I don't want to be married in a church, but I do want David to marry me.' I had to tell her that I was no longer registered as a celebrant, but that I certainly would have if I could. I had not heard of, or from, the family since her daughter was a child. As we talked on her mother said, 'I have often thought that I would not have retained my sanity during the children's adolescent years, if it had not been for seeing and hearing you each week.' If love is made real in one moment of our life, it remains real forever.

This was the foundation of Jesus' teaching. In writing about it, I have explored its nature. Love takes many forms, shaped by the people who surround us. The centre of his teaching concerns our human relationships. A great deal of it concerns our necessary involvement in a society controlled by law. He teaches that living by law, while necessary, has inherent dangers and by its nature cannot promote a loving life. I have explored the relationship between the two and related it to the life of the early Christian Church as it developed its doctrine and institutional form. I have argued that the basic error in that process was to maintain the concept of, and belief in, the existence of a supernatural God who created the world and chose the nation of Israel to fulfil His purpose by adhering to His divine law. This led to a distorted view of the life and teaching of Jesus and the development of doctrine that contradicted it.

As stated previously, I do not advocate the creation of a new Church. The mainstream Christian Churches, despite the errors that I have written about, have retained the kernel of the teaching. I maintain, however, that increasing numbers of Church adherents have been alienated from it by its authoritarian structures, its irrelevant rituals, its corrupted teaching and its imposed morality.

Finally, I have suggested a possible outline of a Church ordered by love and not by law. Against a background of nearly two thousand years of institutionalism, this seems an impossible dream.

Dreams, however, can be glimpses of the future. I have written about dreams and disappointments; I have known both. Looking back, I realise that I have not only glimpsed the dreams I have had, but lived them. The dream is the reality. It is what Jesus called 'eternal life', the life I am living now.

Appendices

November 2013, twenty-two months after David's death, saw two celebratory public occasions held at Toorak Uniting Church. The first, on the afternoon of Sunday 17 November, was a concert titled *The Golden Years of Musical Comedy 1845–1928*. The program of popular music from the Victorian and Edwardian eras to the Roaring Twenties was devised by Torquil Syme, a friend and student of mine. The delightful concert of singing and dancing was given in costume by a group of talented performers, mostly my students, and followed by refreshments. This was the first of the many fundraising concerts for Uniting AgeWell's Music For David program.

Four days later, on the evening of Thursday 21 November, the book *Love Made Real: David Hodges' Service to the Church and Community* was launched. I compiled this book on David's ministry at Toorak Uniting Church and the community outreach programs he initiated there. The book includes some of David's writings and sermons, and memories of him from family members and friends. The Reverend Dr Francis Macnab AM officially launched the book; David's younger daughter, Jeannie, spoke on behalf of his family; and songs were performed by friends Catriona De Vere and Chris van Raay. Chris, with his skills in layout and graphic design, was also significantly involved in the publication of this book and *Making Love Real*.

Three former staff members from Uniting AgeWell's Carer Respite Service attended the book launch: Dee Parfrey (the then Manager, who devised the name 'Music For David'), Jenny Linossier and Nyree Shandley, all of whom were actively involved in establishing Music For David. Jenny and Nyree gave an enlightening audiovisual presentation of the work of what was then a pilot project, later the Music For David program.

As is the case with David's book *Making Love Real*, any money made over the years from the sale of the book *Love Made Real* has been given to Uniting AgeWell for the work of its Music For David program.

David Ross-Smith

The Gift of Music

The beautiful 'Music For David' logo was designed by our friend David Hubble. He has used musical symbols and the image of our favourite Australian native plant, the Telopea speciosissima. *Red, symbolising the energy of life, love and courage, was David's favourite colour; green symbolises healing, growth and renewal.*

'Music For David' was inspired by the dementia experience of the late The Reverend David Hodges AM and his partner David Ross-Smith who cared for him. Their shared love of music brought each joy and comfort and played a significant part in David's care. Uniting AgeWell's relationship with them commenced in 2011 through our Carer Respite Service.

At David Hodges' service of thanksgiving in February 2012, donations were received for his book *Making Love Real*. This memorial gift became the foundation of the Music For David program offered by Uniting AgeWell ever since; its continuance has been largely due to the overwhelming passion, energy and generosity of David Ross-Smith and the commitment to the program of members of our Carer Respite Service.

David, together with family, friends and supporters, have raised considerable funds to support the program. Fittingly, it has been achieved through music, with concerts and soirées organised each year by David and friends, featuring some of Australia's finest musicians and singers who have been inspired to volunteer their talents — gifts for which we are extremely grateful.

The Music For David program provides short-term respite for carers of people with dementia, through the use of programmed music playlists and the support of a music therapist.

The program has evolved as technology has improved and changed. Initially using an iPod shuffle and headphones, this has advanced to cordless mp4-enabled headphones, specialised apps on a tablet, and speakers or headphones. Regardless of the technology, the core has always been music significant to each individual, and equipment that best fits their needs.

Music For David music therapist, Winifred Beevers, says the most rewarding part of this program is hearing and seeing the responses of our clients. As they listen to their music, their eyes light up, they smile and relax. Some hum or sing along, while others tap their fingers or feet in time to the music. And while this is happening, their carers get a welcome break, are able to accomplish other household tasks or simply get time to relax and enjoy some quiet time.

Clients have listened to their music to alleviate anxiety and agitation while waiting for medical appointments, being driven in the car, in the early evening as a meal is prepared, while in hospital, when in respite care and in many other situations.

Funds received for Music For David enabled Uniting AgeWell to expand music therapy services to include live group sessions in one of our day centres in 2015 and, more recently in 2020, to provide individual in-home sessions accessed through our Home Care Packages program. Continuing the tradition of adapting technology to suit the client, and in response to the COVID-19 pandemic, these sessions are now using teleconferencing software.

This wonderful program started as a memorial for David Hodges. It has become a testament to his relationship with David Ross-Smith and the music they shared.

On behalf of Uniting AgeWell and the many people who have benefitted from Music For David, our heartfelt thanks and deep appreciation.

Rebecca Ryan
General Manager, Marketing &
Community Relations,
Uniting AgeWell

Winifred Beevers
Registered Music Therapist,
Music For David program
Uniting AgeWell

Donations to the Music For David program can be made via the following link, where you can click on a dropdown list labelled 'Select donation cause' to select the option 'Music For David':

https://unitingagewell.org/donate

Memorials for David's Ministry

By way of introduction, I am using words, written by Tasma Wischer, with the title 'A Man for All Seasons'. These words were printed in the order of service used at the Service of Thanksgiving for David, held at Toorak Uniting Church on Wednesday 1 February 2012. Tasma is a friend, former staff member and long-time participant in the life of the Church.

David Ross-Smith

A MAN FOR ALL SEASONS
Some said David should have been an architect or a builder. He was both: a creative innovator in concrete and abstract forms, and light years ahead of his time. In his own words he 'made love real'. Many of us here today received his wise counsel in both sad and happy times. We may not remember his words, but we still hear his voice: the gentle tone, the twinkle of warmth and humour in the eye, and the knowledge in our hearts that hope and just being there for others can save and heal. We thank David for all the words, the baptisms, the marriages, the funerals and all the love in between.

Hodges Room at Scots Church, Adelaide, 2019

[Catriona Milne, David's eldest child and elder daughter, prepared the following. She spoke on behalf of the Hodges family during the service at Scots Church, Adelaide, when the memorial to David, the Hodges Room, was dedicated.]

Our father, David, was a leader of people, and through his work created lasting change. Following Dad's death in 2012, people have been moved to honour his service by dedicating a space in his name at two of the places he loved, Scots Church in Adelaide, and Toorak Uniting Church in Melbourne. Having a place of remembrance acknowledges his work and is perhaps a way of saying 'thanks'.

While Dad shunned public praise and may have felt ambivalent about being remembered this way, there were many people for whom this was an important tribute, and he would have understood that.

On Sunday 9 August 2015, the service at Toorak Uniting Church, conducted by its minister, The Reverend Dr Christopher Page, was a celebration of Dad's ministry and included the naming of the Hodges Gallery in its Kinross Arts Centre.

At the celebration, Jeannie, the youngest of Dad's four children spoke about Dad and ended her speech with this reflection:

> While it is important to reflect and remember the work that Dad did, we hope that this memorial will continue to serve as a reminder of the principles by which Dad lived: that there is good

in everyone, that we are all capable of great things, and it is up to all of us to create the community in which we wish to live, through hard work and perseverance.

Although Dad left Scots Church, Adelaide, in 1968, there were several people there who remembered him and, fifty-one years later, in 2019, wanted his contribution to be honoured. Meg Butler was one of these people. Over several months the idea took shape and it was decided to name a room after Dad. The following words were used to describe him:

> An inspirational and visionary leader. He was a friend, mentor and counsellor to many with a powerful and wide-ranging intellect.

The Hodges Room used to be Dad's office and is now the headquarters in South Australia and the Northern Territory of *The Big Issue*. This is 'an independent, not-for-profit organisation that develops solutions to help homeless, disadvantaged and marginalised people positively change their lives.' Their work is very much in keeping with Dad's practice throughout his ministry of involving the Church in the community by setting up programs of social outreach.

Family members travelled to Adelaide to join the congregation for the morning service on Sunday 13 October 2019. The service, conducted by its minister, The Reverend Dr Peter Trudinger, included some of David's favourite hymns. Morning tea followed with a warm and heartfelt speech from Meg Butler who gave a chronology of Dad's life, interwoven with some of her own memories where she described the significant impact he has had on her life.

Hodges Gallery, Kinross Arts Centre, Toorak Uniting Church, 2015

[On Sunday 9 August 2015 there was a service at Toorak Uniting Church, which celebrated David's ministry there with the dedication of a memorial. The service was conducted by the minister, The Reverend Dr Christopher Page, and contained beautiful organ and choral music and hymns that David loved. Two friends spoke eloquently about David and his ministry — Tim Brown during the service, and June DeVere in the Kinross Arts Centre where, during the reception, she made a speech dedicating the Hodges Gallery. David's younger daughter, Jeannie, spoke on behalf of the Hodges family, as did I as his partner. Many friends and family joined the congregation for this celebration of David's life and ministry.

Afterwards, some family members and friends came to our home for a lunch of his favourite meal — fish and chips!

The Hodges Gallery was originally the formal sitting room in the manse where the Hodges family lived for most of David's ministry in Toorak. The following is Jeannie's speech given in the Hodges Gallery.]

This room is a special room. It has always been a special room. It was the room where the dinner guests would retire for coffee and port, and I would peek in the door and eavesdrop on the conversation. It was the room that housed the piano; it was the room where Mum and Dad would talk of serious matters; it was the room where the best furniture was kept; and where we gathered for special occasions. It was the room in which I curtsied to the Governor-General and nearly fell over.

And now it is special as it bears the name of a good man, our Dad. But what does this memorial mean, what are we remembering Dad for?

I believe if I asked every one of you what you feel Dad would best be remembered for, you would mention the word 'leader'. Just recently, I read that a leader was someone 'who saw something that needed doing and did it'. A simple definition, but one that resonates strongly with the type of man Dad was. Catriona recently looked at this church's monthly planner from the early 1980s and was staggered at the number of groups and activities timetabled for each week: discussion groups, dancing groups, music, RAP [a human relations training course for young people], activities for older people, just to name a few. Catriona was particularly interested to see groups to support refugees, a demonstration of how far-sighted Dad was. His ability to get things done created a foundation upon which the church continues to flourish.

Of course, Dad was not alone in realising the vision of a vibrant Church based on strengthening community and social justice. Dad was a powerful orator in the pulpit and was equally persuasive in his day-to-day interactions. He would seem to effortlessly bring individuals and the church administration with him on a trajectory of change with skill and sensitivity. Dad was great at choosing people to do jobs that would extend them just enough. His belief in the goodness and competence of people, and his ability to guide with quiet understanding and trust, enriched the lives of so many. Dad would never seek to impose his will; he would encourage, teach and model what he thought was the right thing to do.

Despite Dad's ability to lead and his influential and charismatic presence both within and outside of the church community, he was fundamentally a shy man who in some ways was unaware of the degree of influence he had over others. He was humble, not because he thought it was good to be so, but because he found being prideful profoundly uncomfortable.

If there is one thing we would like Dad to be remembered for it would be his warmth and kindness. Dad loved people and people loved Dad. If some of you were at the memorial service following his death, you will recall me talking about my memory of watching him with a frightened, confused homeless man who sought comfort from him. This man was just one of many hundreds who sought solace and were given time, respect and comfort, as well as food and shelter. Bill Williams, a theologian with cystic fibrosis who died in 1998 writes, 'I've been with people who are not made anxious by my brokenness, and I've seen the difference. It is in fact the best definition of ministry I have ever heard, it so defined what I needed. Engrave this upon your forehead if you wish to do good. Ministry is a non-anxious presence. You can tell such grace by its care, by its attentive ear, by its pace.' This was how Dad lived his life.

On behalf of myself, Catriona, Chris, Alastair and Mum, who could not be here today, we would like to thank David and the church for creating this memorial for Dad. While it is important to reflect and remember the work Dad did, we hope the memorial will continue to serve as a reminder of the principles by which Dad lived: that there is good in everyone, that we are all capable of great things, and it is up to all of us to create the community in which we wish to live, through hard work and perseverance.

David's children, Alastair, Catriona, Chris and Jeannie, at the dedication of the Hodges Gallery.

The Reverend David McIndoe Hodges AM, B.A. (Melb.), B.D. (Edin.)

David on Sunday 25 September 1983 — the day of his retirement from Toorak Uniting Church and full-time ministry.

Born in Melbourne on 9 January 1924, David Hodges was educated at Malvern Boys' Grammar School and Scotch College. After he left school, he enlisted in the Australian army (A.I.F.) in 1942 to serve in World War II. Following his discharge, he completed an arts degree at the University of Melbourne, majoring in English and philosophy, then commenced a Diploma of Education.

He left Australia in 1949 for Edinburgh, Scotland. At New College, The University of Edinburgh, he completed a degree in divinity in which his major was New Testament studies. He graduated *magna cum laude* and was awarded the Gunning Prize when he topped his year. He considered studying for a Doctor of Philosophy but decided that this was unnecessary for his chosen career in parish ministry. During this time, he was a student assistant at St Giles' Cathedral and was licensed there as a minister of the Church of Scotland in 1952.

David was invited to become assistant to the minister of the Scots' Church, Melbourne, and on his return to Australia was ordained a minister of the Presbyterian Church of Australia. During the next thirty years, he ministered to three congregations: St Andrew's, Bairnsdale; Scots Church, Adelaide; and Toorak Presbyterian, later Uniting Church.

In 1967 he was moderator-elect in South Australia, but did not take up the position when he was called to Toorak in 1968.

Always committed to the ecumenical movement, he helped create partnerships at Toorak with the Anglican and Roman Catholic Churches — the Toorak Ecumenical Movement. The Toorak Ecumenical Opportunity Shop was born from this collaboration. He was involved in the early discussions that led to planning for the union of the Methodist and Presbyterian Churches and the Congregational Union. He was appointed a member of the Joint Commission that was charged with the task of writing the Basis of Union.

David was convener of Presbyterian Social Services in Victoria from 1969 until the creation of the Uniting Church in 1977. In the years immediately prior to Union, he was chairman of the steering committee, consisting of representatives from each Church, charged with preparing a report and recommendations for the creation of the Uniting Church Social Services. This was adopted at the first Uniting Church of Australia Synod (Victoria) in 1977. After Union he continued as chairman of Canterbury Family Centre and as a member of the board of St Andrew's Hospital.

In 1977 David was awarded the Queen's Silver Jubilee Medal for outstanding service in his field of work.

In 1981 he was invited to become guest preacher for two months at Madison Avenue Presbyterian Church in New York. In 1982 he decided to retire from full-time ministry and from his position as minister of Toorak Uniting Church. [His decision to retire prematurely was made to protect his family and the church's congregation from any gossip and criticism created by the public knowledge of our relationship. In the 1980s homophobia and prejudice were rife and exacerbated by the AIDS crisis.]

In 1983 David was made a Member of the Order of Australia (AM) in recognition of his 'services to religion and the community'.

David at Government House, Melbourne, after receiving his Order of Australia, 1983.

Following his retirement in 1983, he was for twelve years chairman of Trading Partners, a not-for-profit company that imported handicrafts, principally from small groups in developing countries, and retailed them in Victoria. He also conducted many weddings and funerals, served several congregations as a locum minister and, in 1998, was acting presbytery minister for the Presbytery of Nepean. David also met requests for counselling and, from the mid-1980s, served as a volunteer telephone counsellor for AIDS-Line during the worst period of the AIDS epidemic.

David's interest in architecture and design led to the renovation of a number of houses, and with his long-time partner, David Ross-Smith, the building of three new homes. The second of these was in Sherbrooke in the beautiful Dandenong Ranges outside Melbourne, where his lifelong interest in landscaping and gardening was given ample scope. The third house, in Glen Iris, was built with skill and care by David's elder son, Chris, in 2003.

Dementia, chronic pain and physical frailty affected the last years of David's life. However, he accepted these changes with characteristic dignity and patience and remained constant in his love for others. He died peacefully at home in Glen Iris on the morning of 22 January 2012, with his two daughters, Catriona and Jeannie, and partner, David, by his side. During the period of terminal palliative care prior to his death, David's love, trust and 'non-anxious presence' were inspirational, creating an experience of 'making love real' for all those present and involved in this last phase of his life.

On 5 April 2012, Holy Thursday, an obituary written by David's younger son, Alastair, was published in *The Sydney Morning Herald* and *The Age* newspapers. It was given the title: 'Gifted preacher inspired strength.'

After the service of thanksgiving for David at Toorak Uniting Church, on 1 February 2012, copies of his book *Making Love Real* were made available for people to take and, if they wished, they could make a donation towards supporting people living with dementia and those caring for them. The money received was given to Uniting AgeWell — the aged-care services of the Uniting Church. This gift became the foundation of Uniting AgeWell's 'Music For David', a music program that supports people in their homes who are living with dementia, and provides temporary respite for their carers.

Memorials have been created at two churches in recognition of David's ministry there. On Sunday 9 August 2015, the 'Hodges Gallery' was dedicated at Toorak Uniting Church, Melbourne, in its Kinross Arts Centre; and on Sunday 13 October 2019, the 'Hodges Room' was dedicated at Scots Church, Adelaide.

David is held in loving memory and gratitude by many — especially his expanding family, friends and partner, David Ross-Smith.

The Reverend David McIndoe Hodges AM

www.ingramcontent.com/pod-product-compliance
Lightning Source LLC
Chambersburg PA
CBHW020321010526
44107CB00054B/1924